THE
TROUBLE
WITH

AMERICA

THE
TROUBLE
WITH
AMERICA

Michel Crozier

Translated by Peter Heinegg

Foreword by David Riesman

UNIVERSITY OF
CALIFORNIA PRESS
Berkeley   Los Angeles   London

105488

University of California Press
Berkeley and Los Angeles, California

University of California Press, Ltd.
London, England

Copyright © 1984 by The Regents of the University of California

Library of Congress Cataloging in Publication Data

Crozier, Michel.
  The trouble with America.

  Rev. translation of: Le mal américain.
  Includes index.
  1. United States—Civilization—1945-
2. National characteristics, American. I. Title.
E169.12.C7613 1984   973.92   84-2549
ISBN 0–520–04978–0

Printed in the United States of America

1 2 3 4 5 6 7 8 9

For my American friends of the fifties and sixties,
whose enthusiasm and daring made me question
my own country, and for my American students of the
late sixties, seventies, and eighties, whose skepticism
and anxiety made me question *their* country,
this book of questions, in payment of a debt.

CONTENTS

FOREWORD

David Riesman

MICHEL CROZIER HOPES that *The Trouble with America* will help the country he loves and admires to become more responsive to what he regards as its best imperatives. The United States does frighten him as much as it frightens this writer and other Americans and many Europeans. We are frightened by the periodically subdued provocativeness vis-à-vis the Russians and their client states and by the pursuit, through seeking to build an impregnable defense, of a first-strike nuclear policy. What makes Crozier anxious is the cultural and economic consequences for the United States and for the planet of American political, industrial, and intellectual stagnation. To be sure, there are lessons in the book for the French, concerning whose industrial stalemate and bureaucratic *immobilisme* Crozier has also written. But the main concern is with America. That is very different from Alexis de Tocqueville, who hoped through *Democracy in America* to teach his French conservative or reactionary friends that the United States, and correspondingly democracy, were viable, equitable, though sadly mediocre polities and modes of life. As Cushing Strout once put it, he was thinking of France while looking at America.

Crozier came to the United States right after World War II in 1946 when he was twenty-five years old. Leaving a shattered France, he writes of himself as of that time: "I was a pro-American leftist, a somewhat rare species in France, but one that still could be respectable." He was here for the Henry Wallace campaign in 1948. He was captivated by the America he discovered. He observed many situations and potentials from which French elites could learn in America, and from which engineers, businessmen, and others then proceeded to learn. *The Trouble with America* begins with a discussion of those early buoyant years, with their high expectations, and then proceeds to the current "trouble," which poses the question as to whether a democracy as large, legalistic, and moralistic as the American is governable and capable of incremental change.

The America Crozier sought out on his first visit was the spirited and gregarious one of the labor organizer. He describes in detail his meeting with an old union activist (perhaps David Dubinsky), too old to go to the forthcoming United Auto Workers meeting in Atlantic City, who instructed Crozier: "You have to get to know the country. New York, Washington, that's not America. . . . Discover how huge this country is." Crozier followed the organizer's advice. He found the UAW a center of union idealism. The big unions even supported the generosity of the Marshall Plan. He noted that America's labor rhetoric was then and remains very much less poisonously hate-filled than that of Europe.

Attractively new to Crozier was the emphasis on negotiation and bargaining. "And civilization began with *Robert's Rules of Order* . . . armed with his manual, a good chairman could squelch troublemakers [at the faculty meetings I attend, "troublemakers" know the *Rules* and chairmen are diffident]." Implicit in the insistence on collective bargaining was a naive but marvelously humane confidence in the power of speech: as long as one keeps talking, one is bound to find a solution. Implicit is the judgment that the bosses are not monsters, and that if they can be made to listen, they too will bargain (p. 6). The very term "business agent" rather than "labor organizer" sounds odd to a Frenchman.

There are side glances back to France; for example, the news that English is the language of choice at the new French business school near Fontainebleau. He writes of himself that, like other Europeans, he was at first impressed by American openness. "Those Americans who so often seem incoherent mumblers communicate infinitely better than the French, who are so proud of their artful self-expression" (p. 133). There followed a period of seeing American relationships as superficial—the quick smile of the salesman. Only later does he appreciate that Americans search for complex human relationships, but find doing so difficult, with any code in a permissive, mobile, and volatile society absent or uncertain.

That volatility is one of the principal themes of the book, which does not pretend to analyze *the* trouble, but to diagnose some troubles. Having seen the unions at first with perhaps a shade too idealistic a vision, he now regards them the way many disappointed liberals do, as conservative where not corrupt, and as obsessed with bargaining, procedure, and legalistic forms that impede productivity and cannot possibly promote the quixotic goals of equality and justice.

I believe that many Americans will be most surprised by Crozier's impassioned critique of what he calls "the delirium of due process." This writer shares much of Crozier's concern with the negative consequences in an individualistic society of everyone's claiming "rights," and also claiming "rights" as members of an ethnic or minority group. Rights of this sort cannot be handled by negotiation or compromise; they are moral abstractions codified in bureaucratic procedure and through litigation. The traditional game of negotiation, that is, the collective bargaining of the unions, is " . . . crystallized into a truly religious movement in which each particular struggle seemed to grow out of a single sacred cause."

One of the "rights" is to penetrate the secrets of those in authority, toward whom there is now a cynicism in America even greater than the habitual skepticism of the French concerning the graduates of the *Grandes Écoles* who presume to govern them. In America in the past "bulwarks of authority, distance, and secrecy have protected those in charge of maintaining peace and leading the commonwealth." Today, having made a scapegoat of Richard Nixon rather than endure cheating in so virtuous a democracy, America has seen its structures break down; these structures cannot exist without at least a minimum amount of tolerance for secrecy. In place of leaders, we have celebrities. Woodward and Bernstein are the heroes of a melodrama.

In addition to discovering on his first visit the new breed of business agents, among whom he was treated as a brother and taken to bars for eager, breezy talk and beer, Crozier discovered the universities, and particularly the newly buoyant and optimistic social scientists. Like himself, many had become sociologists in the hope of bringing about rational, peaceful change in society (he does not allow for those who entered academic life to get their revenge on society). Crozier appreciates how millennial were the early hopes of planners of the Great Society, along with their academic advisers and supporters. He regards it as no less quixotic for anyone to have believed that it was possible to conduct a rational, limited war in Vietnam, knowing virtually nothing about the country, its history and its peoples.

When Crozier turns his attention to contemporary America, he sees the earlier hopes not so much chastened as turned into a soured individualism. To be sure, President Reagan singing "Happy Days are Here Again" is dreaming, like the Marxists, that one can get rid of history. American youth, however, seems to be singing another song.

American education engrosses Crozier, as it has other observers. The universities seem to him as dispirited or even mean spirited as the unions seem encrusted. It dismays him that students have turned in on themselves. They seem far less curious about the world than they were at the time of his first visit. "Never before have young people been so self-centered and America-centered." He regards American youth in general as precocious, quickly anticipating adulthood, but in other ways as remaining adolescent in being insufficiently socialized, unwilling to participate in community building and preferring what he terms individualistic "affirmative action" as a form of self-protection. He writes, "When every group has access, one way or another, to every decision, one should not be surprised that the upshot is confusion and erratic choices. When everybody is free to go in and out everywhere without shouldering the least responsibility in return, when there is no social or cultural barrier to straighten out the chaos in negotiations, long-term policies are no longer feasible." Even the spread of knowledge is put to use in giving individuals "the luxury of displaying a fine intransigence." Crozier describes his experience in asking Harvard students to give an example of a significant innovation, only to discover that those they can think of have negative consequences, or perhaps some sort of trick. With the overt disappearance of what Crozier terms America's "demon virtue," these students are now more resigned than French students.

In his judgment, the new frontier for America lies in thinking, in intellectual effort, which implies investment in the institutions that make knowledge and understanding feasible. It dismays him that many of the best students go into law, fueling the delirium of due process, or go into business without training in science and technology. Some of these concerns will not be unfamiliar to American readers. The same holds for Crozier's judgment that improvement in the educational process requires putting excellence in learning ahead of justice in allocation of places and results. He sees litigation as a form of negative participation, the very contrary of the earlier American spirit of voluntary participation which Tocqueville so admired. Correspondingly, Crozier regrets the abandonment of the PTA by career women who are forming their own interest groups. Moreover, the schools as major community enterprises are caught in civil war. Voluntary associations have become, in his judgment, not a set of networks that tie people together, but barricades for self-defense by splintered interest groups, many of them anxious, and ready to be mobilized for reactionary—or, I would add, symbolic—crusades.

Crozier is, however, impressed by American management and by the human relations school of management at the Harvard Business School, along with its virtuoso teaching by the case method. He also appreciates the work of such policy-oriented social psychologists as those he found right after World War II at the University of Michigan, who, like Rensis Likert and Dorwin Cartwright, contended that if people are well treated and warmly responded to, they will conduct themselves reciprocally. He admires them for their experimental outlook and lack of cynicism, although he is himself skeptical of any belief in the fundamental goodness of human nature.

Crozier's America does not include the South. He nowhere deals with the blockages created by federalism as such, but treats the whole country, as many Americans do today, simply as a nation-state. It is a largely secular and cosmopolitan America that he is looking at. When he turns to foreign policy, he sees the Cuban missile crisis as Kennedy's and America's triumph. (In my judgment he does not appreciate the damage done to Khrushchev's reputation in the Soviet Union, leading to his displacement by the less open, less imaginative, and more repressive Brezhnev & Co.; a more mature, less brash American leadership could have handled the situation in a fashion less humiliating to Khrushchev. Nor does he see that crisis as an element in the very American hubris which troubles him in the Reagan administration.)

In the final chapter, "The Challenge Ahead," Crozier discusses the negative outcomes of what have been regarded as the American successes, whether in due process as a system, or in the mass production, mass consumption market or in the egalitarian welfare state: these very advances, when congealed, have become the sources of decline. Previous successes in meeting change have left America with a metaphysic that is unadapted to the present crisis. For example, the protests by environmentalists and others which slow down or even block nuclear power (astonishing to the French in whose country, in the absence of antitrust laws, all nuclear plants have been built to the same careful specifications) are based on the belief that only principles should count and that, whatever the long-term public interest, people should be encouraged to insist on their rights in a completely unilateral fashion.

If I have suggested that *The Trouble with America* resembles the plaintive song of a disappointed admirer, I would give a wrong impression. Crozier remains an exuberant explorer. He does see the United States as suffering long-term consequences from its sclerotic legalism, its hostility to organization, its worship of the Constitution (an assertion I am inclined to doubt—if we continue to tinker with the Constitution, we may find ourselves repealing the Bill of Rights quite readily). His curiosity about the United States, in all aspects within his purview, remains.

Crozier cares, but he does not preach. He illuminates his vision of what might some day become an only incrementally expansive and manageably reformed America. More the searcher and less the reformer than he was in 1946, Crozier hopes that he will be listened to by thoughtful Americans, and that his book might make a bit of difference in how we see ourselves and hence how we might behave. I share that hope.

PREFACE

IWROTE THE FRENCH VER-
sion of this book at a fever
pitch, fresh from a teaching
experience at Harvard in the Spring semester of 1980. I had taught
there before but had not been back since 1970. This new visit came
as a shock. Everything I saw, everything I lived through was so much
at odds with what I had come to expect from a country I felt I knew
in depth and from within.

Many things have happened since that gloomy Spring of 1980,
a season that appears in retrospect as the lowest ebb of the American
mood. In certain ways the country has rebounded during four years
of the Ronald Reagan administration, but the rebound seems to be
more rhetoric than reality. Basic problems have not changed. The
questions I had asked when writing three years ago are still relevant
and still worth debating now.

This book, however, was written not only in French but for a
French audience. Its translation raised a host of irritating minor prob-
lems. I had explained many specific features of American life for the
French reader, using analogies and comparisons that drew heavily on
French political culture and folklore. A fairly basic background had

to be provided to make American events understandable in France, and I tried to provide it. In this translation, however, I have suppressed these French references as much as I could.

To be specific, I have suppressed four chapters that did not seem relevant for the presentation in America of the main argument of the book. In them, I tried to convey to the French public the traumatic quality and the deep meaning for the American psyche of the years of sound and fury that stretch from J. F. Kennedy's assassination to the return of the hostages from Teheran. In so doing, however, I related a story all too well known in the United States in a cursory way and in terms that could make sense for the French political tradition. Here, I have replaced those chapters with a short essay: "*Will Happy Days Be Here Again?*" In this chapter and in a new conclusion, I have tried to retain some of this historical reflection without actually presenting once again the events.

What I have not suppressed at all is the bent or logic of the original writing, central to which is the spontaneous wondering of Europeans at American idiosyncrasies. I ask my American readers to bear with this seeming naivete, for it has a point. Americans could do worse than learn when and why they make Europeans scratch their heads.

The new addition of this book was made possible by a grant from the Woodrow Wilson International Center for Scholars, Washington, D.C. While the statement and views expressed herein are those of the author and are not necessarily those of the Wilson Center, I do wish to give my heartfelt thanks to the Wilson Center for their generous support. I wish to thank equally the University of California, Irvine, for providing support during the last period of my work.

M. C.

The University of California, Irvine
February 1984

INTRODUCTION

FROM THE VERY BEGIN-
ning, America, the land of
freedom, has been Eu-
rope's dream: a society built on new foundations, held together not
by tradition but by principle, a generous, hospitable country, open to
the most daring experiences.

Just as people used to say, "Every man has two homelands, his
own and France," I myself feel I have two homelands, France and
that dreamed-of America. And I am not the only one. Many Frenchmen, many Europeans (including those conforming to the rather
hypocritical, if often fashionable, anti-Americanism) would have to
make a similar admission.

I knew the old, happy America, the home of progress and public
trust. During my first visit in 1947–1948, I was won over by its irresistible appeal. I had come, still a very young man, to write a book on
American labor unions. Thanks to a scholarship I was able to live in
the country for fifteen months. And what I found was hope, for this
was the land of hope. The people believed so deeply and so sincerely
in unlimited social progress, free from violence and revolution, fueled
only with sincere dialogue, that only barbarians could reject them. I

was also impressed by the generous international spirit that led to something too often forgotten since then; namely, to the Marshall Plan and the reconstruction of Europe.

I came back to America in 1956, again in 1959–1960, and every year after that, occasionally for long stays to teach or to do research. One after another I acquainted myself with the various sectors of American society, all swayed by the same enthusiasm, the same generosity, the same illusory ideal of perfection. First I explored academic, intellectual America, with its think tanks and prestigious universities, where the rites of truth—that supremely modern cult invented and then forgotten by Europe—were still celebrated. Later, in the early sixties, I stumbled onto America-the-decision-maker, a country haunted by a still more dangerous dream, the dream of a kind of rationality that could burn away the fog of conflicting interests and passions. This America, whose virtues Jean-Jacques Servan-Schreiber hymned to us in his *American Challenge*,[1] had already been dealt a lethal blow. But nobody knew that yet, neither I nor anyone else.

From 1970 to 1980 I had no further opportunities to teach in America. When I returned in the spring of 1980 to give a course at Harvard, I experienced a terrible shock. Everything was the same, and yet everything was different: what had changed was the meaning. The dream had faded, leaving behind nothing but empty rhetoric. University communities and young people were demoralized, the unions were trapped in a routine of increasingly fruitless negotiations, decision-makers had lost their grip on reality, the economy was adrift, the big corporations were bogged down in their own bureaucracy, information was buried beneath an avalanche of computer printouts, statistics even from the Bureau of Census were no longer reliable. The whole country seemed to have lost its bearings.

To be sure, I had been aware of the problems. I had lived through the Vietnam era, the time of riots and unrest, the madness of Watergate. But I too went on thinking of the United States as inexhaustible, always capable of coming up with new resources. Suddenly I realized that the limits had been reached. From now on America would be an old country, like the others, trying to find its way. In barely a single generation a profound change had taken place.

While Europe and Japan were developing, America was slipping into stagnation, and despite appearances its influence in world affairs was on the wane. Figures, of course, have to be taken for what they

---

[1]Jean-Jacques Servan-Schreiber, *The American Challenge* (New York: Atheneum, 1968).

are worth, but here are some eloquent ones: in 1950 the average American's standard of living was more than two-and-a-half times higher than that of the average Frenchman or German, five times higher than that of the average Japanese. In the late seventies Continental Europe had more or less caught up and Japan was to do so much more quickly a little later. In the decade of the seventies the average blue collar worker's standard of living declined by 9 percent in America and *rose 75 percent* in France and in Germany! For all its wealth of raw materials, America has suffered more from the oil crisis than Japan, Germany, or even France.

What an extraordinary contrast between the illusions Americans fed on and the results they obtained. Europeans spent their time complaining, but they wanted growth and they got it, in larger measure than they expected. They wanted modernization and they got it. In the struggle against various forms of inequality, the outcome has been disappointing, of course, but by no means negligible, whereas the illusions of Americans have been cruelly dashed. No country has ever made such vast expenditures on social programs with so little to show for it. At times poverty appears to be increasing as fast as the money spent to stop it. Twenty-one million people, or almost 10 percent of the population, were receiving food stamps in 1980. And we find similar failures in every sector of society. The nation that invented management is becoming aware that others are using it to much better advantage. In the land of consensus the late-seventies polls showed that citizens had even less confidence in their public officials and institutions than the French had in the Fourth Republic just before it went under. And world leadership, which seemed so natural to a people proud of their way of life and eager to spread it for the benefit of all humanity, is rapidly becoming no more than a memory.

What happened? How was so striking a turnaround possible? How could a country so rich in material, intellectual, and moral resources founder this way in confusion and disorder? This book is my effort to gain a clearer view of the situation. In it I relate what I have seen and felt, and I ask questions. It is too early for a final synthesis of course, but not too early to begin asking the deeper, more searching questions. When Eisenhower declared, thirty years ago, that France had lost its moral fiber, there was a mighty brouhaha from one end of the country to the other. Eisenhower was wrong, as the French would be wrong when it came their turn to return the compliment to America. Nations are not moral entities and cannot be taken to task like children. Quite the contrary: the proper attitude would be to volunteer help for citizens in distress, whose system has broken down and no longer addresses their needs. Hence, my title, *The Trouble with America,* must not be understood in the sense of a culpable flaw, still less as an intrinsic vice. The American trouble has no more real an existence than the *mal français* allegedly handed down from Philip the Fair and Richelieu.

But something is seriously wrong, that much is certain. The United States seems to be pursued at times by its own private demon. If America today can no longer believe in anything, that may well be because it put too much faith in its models of decision making, its mechanisms of negotiation, and its hallowed institutions, all of which worked perfectly well in an older context but which now look decidedly inadequate. Might not the trouble with America, in the final analysis, come right out of the American dream? This is the question I wish to examine, making use both of my critical distance as a sociologist and a foreigner and of my own firsthand experiences as a frequent and interested visitor.

PART

I

AMERICA'S HAPPY DAYS

*There once was a country that believed in a dream
and thought it would come true on earth.
There once was a happy land that had no history.
There once was a New world. . . .*

CHAPTER ONE

UNION AMERICA

or

the Social Dream

Organizing

THE FIRST AMERICA I CAME to know was dressed in a trench coat and looked like Humphrey Bogart. It was 1947. World War II had just been won—a time of hope, when everything was possible. The American labor movement especially was awash in optimism. The reign of equality and justice was about to begin; the democratic ideal was going to be realized. Union America in those days had a watchword, *organize,* and a hero, *the organizer.* On the screen Humphrey Bogart brought justice to bear, righted wrongs; the organizer did even more. He went to the factory workers not to present them with ready-made solutions but to call them up to speak without the complications of dialectical materialism or the shifting orthodoxies of the "correct line," as in Europe. His message was simple: stick together, unite, get organized, and you will be strong, you will make the decisions.

I ran into this organizer again in 1979, in the film *Norma Rae.* He was almost the same, only a bit too psychoanalyzed to satisfy my memories, an ageless type who had been around, no illusions and no fear, intelligent and almost suffering because of it: Humphrey Bogart,

Albert Camus, the journalist in love with truth, the honest lawyer, the
Greek judge of the film *Z*. . . . In *Norma Rae,* that slightly macho film,
women are on his side. At first they do not understand anything; later
they understand only too well: they become activists, and that's dangerous. Women stand for people, the masses. The organizer is there
to exhort them, then to calm and reassure them. He has the wisdom
of experience: fight not for fighting's sake but to win. And if you
cannot win right away, face the fact without getting discouraged, and
fight for tomorrow, for the kids. The struggle has its own wisdom.

Organize—the word was everywhere, the slogan staring out from
column after column in union newspapers, the banner flapping in
the wind at meetings and picnics. Toward the end of the 1940s unionized America provided a healthy share of the world's hope. In that
phase of uncertainty, after the catastrophe had ended and before the
cold war had begun, the great nation that had saved Europe offered
us, along with its factories and its way of life, the vision of a better
world.

The French in that period were desperately skeptical, and I had
come to America, not out of enthusiasm or idealism but simply to see.
I had the feeling that something important was in the works.

I traveled across the length and breadth of the country for fourteen months, attending small meetings and large rallies, talking to
rank and file union members and to organizers. I conducted some
five or six hundred interviews, and I never tired of it. I developed
an inexhaustible capacity for meeting people and explaining things.
I stayed in the United States until Harry Truman's election in November 1948. I shall always remember the black taxi driver in New
York who told me the morning after the tallies were in, "It's a miracle,
sir," as he wept for joy. It was a great day for the unions, the first and
last election they really won, a victory against Henry Wallace's fellow
travelers, Strom Thurmond's southern racists, and Tom Dewey's big
business Republicans.

Working-class America in that epoch displayed a generosity, a
warmth of welcome that I have never encountered anywhere else. It
was the land of openness and goodwill. As long as one did not behave
in a snide, arrogant manner, anybody could walk in anywhere, discuss
the issues with anyone, take part in whatever was going on. I had left
behind me a France—which fortunately has changed, even if many
aftereffects still remain—full of barriers, taboos, and secrets, on the
Left as well as on the Right. Back then one would never dream of
disturbing Monsieur So-and-so or Comrade X so exalted an intellectual, so busy a leader!

In America in 1947 you could call anyone on the phone, even the president. Somebody always answered. I went from city to city, armed with the yellow pages of the telephone directory listing all the unions. I made my appointments: "I'm from France, I'm doing a thesis on unions, can you see me for a moment?" They saw me within the day, if not the hour. Despite my deplorable English, we talked, sometimes for hours at a time, in their offices or over beer in local bars.

In France union militants were always politicians more or less. They sprayed you with quotations and quickly made you feel you had no idea of what was going on. With Americans, by contrast, there was no runaround; you plunged right into the thick of the struggle. Often I had the impression that they had to restrain themselves from talking to me as one of their own: "OK, you see the problem: the boys at General Industries in Wistamazoo are completely in the dark about this, we have to warn them. Good, now you know what's up, you take over." It was action. It was the dawn, the beginning of the world. The people were already mobilized, but there was still work to be done. So you went out there and talked to them. No soft soap, no more or less twisted laws of history, and no outpouring of hatred, either. You brought the simple message of brotherhood: together you will be strong, the boss will not lay down the law any more, there will be no more injustice.

Of course, it was simplistic. It was a myth, and a Christian myth at that. It is no accident that in France today the Confédération Française Démocratique du Travail, with its Christian origins, embodies this myth better than any other union. But myths at certain moments in time can move a mountain or two. I believed this one would.

Negotiating

It was not enough to go out to the people. Once organized, the workers still had to press their claims to a successful finish. Hence another key word for American unionists was *negotiate*. To be sure, working-class America had always believed in the virtues of negotiation which European radicals had so disparaged. But the word had taken on a far more powerful meaning after 1936, which, on both sides of the Atlantic, was a year of large-scale strikes and factory sit-downs (an American invention, by the way). In the early postwar period 1936 was scarcely ten years back. The idea of negotiations leading to victory was as fresh as ever. The people had to get together, to organize, to speak up. Your freedom of speech has been stolen from you. Take it back. That would be the galvanizing slogan of May 1968, but in France all the free speech ended in the kind of uproar that drowns out conversation. In the American working world of 1947, by contrast, speaking up and negotiating came down to the same thing. There was no speech in the abstract; you always spoke to someone, in this case to the boss. Americans had a perhaps naive but marvelously human confidence in the power of speech: as long as you keep talking, you're bound to find a solution. The bosses, naturally, do not want to listen. That's what makes them such bastards. But make them listen and things will work out. After all, they're no monsters.

I no longer remember very clearly what I thought about all that at the time. I was skeptical, of course, and I fought shy of that optimism, but no doubt it made a deep impression on me. This belief in the supremacy of dialogue, when each partner speaks honestly and sincerely, did not, after all, originate with the Americans. It is a profound Christian value that they inherited from Europe. Many years afterward I remembered a story my mother loved to tell me. It happened during World War I, when she was eighteen years old. Her family lived close to the front, and they had a general billeted in the house. Naturally, he enjoyed chatting with the young girl. And one day she spoke up with a vengeance. "General," she said, "do you realize what's going on? You get people, brave soldiers, killed for nothing, and then as if all that never happened, you have the nerve to come here and offer me your chocolates that you order from Paris!" I never learned whether this changed the general in the least, but one never speaks up in vain: fifty or sixty years later the memory of affirming one's dignity remains.

Speaking up, then, immediately suggested holding negotiations. For American workers that word had an almost sacred quality. Very few of them, obviously, had any direct experience in negotiating. Nonetheless they knew all the ins and outs, the preparatory discussions, the data sheets, the preliminary conditions, the quibbling to gain time, the mutual concessions, the snags, the backward slides, the tension, and the long, patient wait. What the workers lived through directly was the background of the discussions: the strike—a catastrophe that was also a holiday and a form of hope. Still they had a feeling for negotiation; it was their business, down to the smallest detail, and it ties in with a dimension of American life whose full importance it took me a while to grasp—the dimension of the law.

To negotiate is to enter the realm of the law. In the eyes of the American worker the boss is not a bastard unless he refuses to negotiate. If he accepts dialogue and respects the law, he may be a decent person. In that case you can get a contract binding both sides, so that the boss will no longer be a dictator. Thus, contracts are vested with a transcendent significance. At the time Americans were demanding a contract as if they were calling for the end of oppression.

It is essential to understand the power of this devotion to negotiation, of this simple, intransigent logic that lay at the very heart of the task of organizing. According to this conception of the labor movement the organizer, in a sense, came to bring civilization. And civilization began with *Robert's Rules of Order*. Electing a chairman, making a motion, asking for cloture—all has to be done by the rules. Apprenticeship to *Robert's Rules* was the transition from savagery to civilization. As long as parliamentary procedure was respected, the communists would try in vain to infiltrate the unions or to demoralize their opponents by dragging meetings out till two o'clock in the morning: armed with his manual, a good chairman could squelch troublemakers. After these rudiments had been mastered, came training sessions in economics and negotiation. I followed many of these "seminars," and remember especially the ones given by my friend Bill, an old organizer who had been at the job for twelve years. He had been through the sitdowns of 1936, he knew all the tricks, and he gave the impression of knowing even more.

We made the rounds of small Michigan cities—Kalamazoo, Jackson, Grand Rapids—and everywhere we went we taught union members the game of negotiation. We divided them up into two groups: bosses and workers. (Curiously, everybody wanted to be a boss. Eventually Bill put me on that side as a matter of course—he thought I was more noncommittal and less vicious than most of the others.) The "workers" itemized their demands, and the "bosses" invariably found the best reasons in the world for turning them down. Bill reworked the whole routine, making comments as he went along. Everyone drank beer and had a lot of fun. This America was genial and amiable, as foreigners often imagined it, a country full of decent folk who do not stint with their time, their money, or their goodwill. It took many years and a lot of traveling before I realized that Americans could be as narrow-minded, nervous, and as stingy as the French, or even worse.

What made Americans seem so generous was, above all, the disparity between them and Europeans in the years from 1945 to 1950. People have forgotten just how sad those years were in Europe when the United States was experiencing one of its happier moments. The mistake was, I think, to attribute this contrast to a basic difference between the dynamism of America and the conservativism of Europe.

Not that this notion was altogether false, but the historical period is crucial here. I might almost compare Americans in that epoch with Frenchmen from the provinces today: even though Paris has not entirely shed its erstwhile anxiety, people in Dijon, Tours, or Périgueux find the time to meet passing strangers and not with their palms up.

A Different Kind of Politics

Even then, in the late forties, it is true, the American labor movement had its problems and inconsistencies. For example, the term *organizer* was in style but it was not used by all union leaders; quite the contrary. Most of the old unions belonging to the American Federation of Labor (AFL) and even some of the newer unions of the Congress of Industrial Organizations (CIO) called their permanent representatives "business agents." The term is far removed from any idealistic connotations, and to a French ear it sounded altogether offensive. The business agent, however, was not simply the product of the conservatism inherent in the old trade unions. He also carried on the ancient and noble tradition of libertarian unionism whereby the workers insist on creating their own union, apart not only from the bosses but also from the politicians. Then, since the members already have their hands full, they hire somebody to represent them. And they have no qualms about collecting dues to pay him or calling him a business agent, exactly as the bosses do. Aren't they worth as much as the bosses? Can't they put on as good a show?

The business agent is a salaried employee who does the bidding of the local union, unlike the European union representative who has authority delegated to him and may tend to abuse it. The figure of the organizer, of course, was much more appealing to European leftists, as it was then to American liberals. He personified movement, conquest, history on the march, whereas the business agent stands for the humdrum world of special interests and contracts: in reality he is just another lawyer. But it must also be noted that the organizer, paid out of headquarters of the parent union—somewhere in New York, Washington, or Detroit—is a functionary, an apparatchik, often an intellectual, whereas the business agent is generally chosen by local members and answers directly to the wishes of his constituency. There is a democratic side to this system, with its more pronounced decentralization and its stronger local roots. Behind all the idealism of the organizer looms the threat of bureaucracy.

In the face of this threat, the response of any dynamic movement is naturally to expand and press forward. Contrary to legend, working class America has always been poorly organized. Despite the power of the major unions, their members have never composed more than one-fourth (now barely 20 percent) of the work force, which is roughly the same as in France but much less than in other European countries. Thus the organizers had some tough battles to fight. The territory was partitioned on a grid, campaign strategies were worked out, the men were even given code names. Each year the CIO launched a fresh assault on the southern textile industry. For years the big New England textile manufacturers had been resettling in the South, where labor was cheap and unions forbidden. Since the South was the chief bastion of the reactionaries, its conquest was supposed to enable all of America to become liberal and progressive. Today, thirty years later, the South is still not much unionized. New offensives continue to be set in motion, minor gains are won here and there, and the whole effort even has the hit film *Norma Rae* to its credit. But the enthusiasm has faded along the way.

In 1948 the movement still believed in victory, because the point was not to bring collective bargaining to a dozen factories but to change the world. American unionists dreamed of a different kind of politics, of brighter tomorrows. The movement was simpler and more concrete than in France, but there, too, workers' hopes were based on a series of wild conjectures.

Politics is a wonderful device for annihilating practical contradictions in a mythical Beyond. Thus, the American labor movement was torn between the old trade unions of the AFL, which were highly selective and more or less racist, and the younger unions of the CIO in the big industries (steel, autos, rubber, electrical equipment), which accepted everyone without restriction as to color or trade. Elsewhere tensions grew between activists and bureaucrats, militants and business agents, shop stewards and national staff members. The Left and the unions were all one in those days, it was the grand dream of an alliance among workers, farmers, blacks, and other minorities. This "crazy quilt," made famous by Franklin Delano Roosevelt, has always been the key to the whole Democratic party strategy. But along with the ethnic minorities in Roosevelt's coalition went a regional "minority," the South, which was indispensable for victory.

The Democratic party, then, the party of movement and change, was anchored by tradition in a region whose instincts were totally opposed to it. (The accession to power of two southern presidents, Lyndon B. Johnson and Jimmy Carter, marks the end, it seems to me, of this classical pattern in American politics.) My union friends dreamed of beating the southern reactionaries and thereby redirecting the Democrats toward a more coherent alliance of all types of oppressed people against the powerful capitalist interests.

Some leftists even argued that there was nothing more to be gained from the Democratic party and that a new labor party had to be founded, on the English model. After all, Eugene Debs's Socialist party had brought out sizable crowds and gotten nearly 1 million votes in 1912.[1] In the twenties Senator Robert La Follette had enjoyed his moment of glory at the head of the Farmer-Labor party, which briefly seemed to threaten the two official parties. Henry Wallace belonged to the same stock. Unfortunately for him and for it, his campaign staff was packed with fellow travelers. And the large unions, which were busy eliminating the many undercover communists and leftists who had infiltrated their ranks during the New Deal, had no intention of accepting the smallest compromise on this point. So they resolutely cast their lot with Harry Truman, whom they quickly came to view as their only recourse in the face of the reactionary, violently anti-union campaign mounted by the Republicans. The secession of the Dixiecrats, who rejected their party's quite moderate platform, reduced still further the base of the old alliance.

The victory in November 1948 was unhoped for, but that "miracle" was not destined to keep any of the promises made by the great dream. Truman was hardly elected when he let bygones be bygones and brought the Southerners back into the party, with all their seniority privileges in committees and their power to block legislation in the Congress. The shadow cast by the extreme leftists had been dispelled, but the problem of rightist Southerners remained. The labor movement dug in for trench warfare.

I Have a Dream

"I have a dream" would be the refrain of Martin Luther King, Jr.'s inspired speech at the Lincoln Memorial in 1963. But by the end of the forties American unionists and liberals were already stirred by a noble vision, which nowadays seems far, far away: universal brotherhood, unshakable unity ("solidarity forever," as they sang in the union hymn), true democracy. And, unlike European leftists (or Richard Nixon), American liberals did not draw up an immense "enemies list." There was Wall Street, of course, the southern reactionaries, the big corporations, but nobody was checking IDs: there was room for every-

[1]Women did not yet have the vote, and America's population was only a third of what it is now. Thus, those million votes carried almost as much weight as the votes garnered by the French Socialist party around the same time.

one in this vision. As for myself, try as I might to resist this somewhat idyllic dream, I could not help feeling profoundly touched by it.

I doubt that I shall ever forget my first convincing lesson in liberal democracy, American style, which I learned from an old gentleman, all shrunken and wrinkled but still smiling. This veteran union lawyer had been a member of the original National Labor Relations Board (which had been decisive in creating the new labor movement) and had arbitrated countless disputes. Late in his life a foundation had given him a grant of two or three hundred thousand dollars, a three-room office in Washington, and a secretary, so that he could spend two years writing a book about his experiences. At the beginning of my first stay in America, I came to see him, unannounced, to ask his advice. He ushered me right in, greeted me very warmly, and with a trace of amusement gave detailed answers to my naive questions. Finally, when I asked him where I could get more material, he said with a gentle smile, "Set yourself up in the next room; there's nobody there, and I've got a collection of all the documents you're looking for."

I came back every day. After a few weeks I was making better sense of the incredible politicojuridical tangle of the American labor movement and beginning to feel an urge to get out of the office. Right around that time the annual conference of the United Automobile Workers was scheduled to take place in Atlantic City, an event of paramount importance in the union world: Walter Reuther, the rising star of unionism, was expected to use the occasion to seize control of the most powerful of all the huge industrial unions. When I announced my intentions of attending, my mentor told me, "Very well, you have to see how that sort of thing works. But you owe me something. I can't go there myself. I'm too old; those big meetings tire me out. So you're going to take notes and report to me." When I protested that I had never written anything in English, he merely laughed. Then, to reassure me, he volunteered the services of his secretary to rearrange my prose. I went to the conference. I was fascinated by the whole enormous circus, I took in every moment of the show—the bravura performances by the stars, conversations in the corridors, tactical sessions of the different caucuses.

I did not have to wait very long after submitting my report, over which I had sweat blood. The old gentleman called me to his office, sat down with me, and after bestowing lavish praise on my fine grasp of the political machinery and maneuvers I had watched, he changed his tone as he added, "But there's something else you still don't understand." He settled back in his chair and looked me right in the

11

eye. "Young man, you'll be leaving soon. That's good, you have to get to know the country. New York, Washington, that's not America. You have to travel, stop along the way, take your time. That's the only way, by seeing how huge this country is, that you'll discover how much this country is a country where everybody has his chance. Look at me. I came from Russia as a little boy with my parents. I took a very long time to understand that when you stay in a corner, you don't get the picture. But afterward I worked, I went everywhere, and I realized that you could do anything, really, anything at all. I'm not pushy, I'm not even ambitious, but I loved to work. And I've had a good life, a full life, more than I ever dared to dream. I owe that to America.

"Young man, don't ever forget this: you're in the land of freedom. And there's another thing you have to know. You're going to stop off in the Midwest and the West, in the states where the Homestead Act applied. You may not know that Congress had required that land be reserved in each state to finance a college. The land grant colleges helped to improve agriculture and later they formed the bases of the state universities. Young people have to be able to study, everybody has to have a chance. Education is freedom, too. It is the new form of freedom. Never forget that, young man; the land of freedom!"

Car People

In 1948, and for a long time afterward, the UAW was the finest embodiment of the American dream. It was the most important union in the CIO, extremely open and active, always in the forefront, culturally and politically. It was run by a dynamic young team, with social-democratic leanings; and it devoted a lot of money and effort to education, that supreme value in "the land of freedom." To understand the peculiar features of this union, one must keep in mind that the automobile industry at the time was a thing unto itself and the auto workers a special breed. The most impressive industry in America was steel, which, together with the railroads and the banks, had produced the first magnates, the Carnegies, the Mellons, the Fricks. Many of the workers in that traditional industry belonged to disciplined minorities—Poles, Italians, Ukrainians. The union had been brought into the steel industry by the miners, who committed all their union funds to the venture and built up a solid, bureaucratic machine. Most of the members were Catholic. It was a quiet operation, rather honest, and not really too supportive of outside causes.

In marked contrast to the mines or steel, the auto industry was, literally and figuratively, a world of mobility. Not only did it sell the means of going from place to place but it was also notable for employee turnover. Henry Ford had offered $5 a day to anyone who showed up for work. There was no paternalism; Ford wanted to be absolute master only during the hours he paid for. And people came from all over the world, including France which never was a country of emigration but which sent quite a number of adventurous people such as the future famous Louis-Ferdinand Céline. Highly skilled jobs required more competent and reliable workers, and they were imported from Europe. Toolmakers, for instance, came from England, Holland, or Germany, and they brought with them their traditions, occasionally libertarian but above all social-democratic.

These men eventually organized the auto union, Walter Reuther and his brothers being the most prominent example. Of the four sons of a strongly social-democratic German working class family who had roamed all around, Walter and Victor had worked in the Soviet Union, in Gorki, which made them, among other things, violently anticommunist. The effort to rebuild the UAW was a mighty one. In weekend seminars, evening courses, and summer schools for union representatives, members received training in economic, health, and pollution problems, as well as in political action and negotiation. Racial problems in those days were harder to deal with. At square dances, whenever it came time to change partners, whites always arranged to switch with other whites, and blacks with other blacks. But it was becoming possible to talk about race and to sow seeds that would sprout later on.

The UAW was a union of virtuous types. Walter Reuther himself had the reputation of never touching a drop of alcohol. In Atlantic City, when they announced the results of the voting delegation by delegation and Reuther's victory was officially proclaimed, someone brought him a beer before he went up to the rostrum and he drank a few gulps. A buzz went through the enormous crowd: "The 'redhead' drinks beer!" Then, on the heels of that extraordinary event, they burst into joyous applause.

For the Whole World

If the labor movement's grand dream had such power, it was undoubtedly made possible by favorable political circumstances, but American expansion all over the world had a lot to do with it, too. The Marshall Plan played an essential role. When General George Marshall, then secretary of state, and President Harry Truman wanted to get their plan through a Congress that was very lukewarm to the idea, they had to lobby round the clock to mobilize the general public and fight off the postwar isolationist reaction, which was threatening to bring the Republicans back into office. So they turned to the unions, the only large popular organization capable of waging that sort of campaign and of preaching international solidarity in all the states of the union.

In the Spring of 1948, in the middle of my long journey—I had followed the advice of my Washington mentor and I was touring the country—I suddenly noticed that wheels were turning. Wherever I went, I was "a brother from France." They insisted I mount the speaker's platform and give speeches. That proved to be easier than anticipated: all I had to do was show myself, say that the French really existed, that they were not antisocial, that they asked only to work and drink beer like the Americans—and they instantly rolled out the red carpet. One day in Cleveland, though, I had a little trouble. I telephoned the business agent of a local metal-workers union. He agreed to see me right away, but I had hardly sat down with him when he started firing: "So you're French. Myself, I don't like your country, not one bit. . . . I was a soldier over there. . . . It's dirty, dirty, and badly organized too. . . . And the people don't like to work. . . . No, I really don't like your country." Arguing as patiently as possible, I managed to score with two examples he had used, concerning poor electric light bulbs and a faulty water pump in Normandy. And, starting with those two pathetic facts, I tried to explain to him what things were like in a country just emerging from years of German occupation and a bitter war. After two hours of discussion and quite a few beers, we were the best of friends. Although I had never had it in mind to ask him about the Marshall Plan, he told me he would vote for it.

But union members in general did not need to be convinced. The Marshall Plan fit in perfectly with their artless generosity, their faith in unlimited progress. As they saw it, people had only to express themselves in order for everyone to understand everyone else. And with the help of education, all men could be equal, they could all be brothers. Granted, union leaders later reaped a profit from these sentiments. Some of them took jobs in Paris and in other European countries, playing to the hilt their role of the liberal wing of American expansion and scandalizing many well-meaning people in the process. Still, it is obvious, if we can view the past critically from a little distance, that the supposed victims of this supposed colonization gained tremendously from it, both in economic and social terms.

The first ones to work their way into the administration of the Marshall Plan were the old troopers of the AFL. They had connections with the CIA and were veterans of the long struggle against the communists. Their top man in France, Irving Brown, directly subsidized the Force Ouvriere union and the Socialist party. Some years later their adversaries in the CIO had their revenge: one of the Reuther brothers settled down in Paris as a competitor, setting himself up in much more austere fashion and shifting ties to the Confederation française des travailleurs chrétiens. To this day the political cultures of the FO and the CFDT, at once analogous and contradictory, still reflect the quarrels and differences their old American friends had between them.

The Other Side of the Coin

One does not negotiate just for the sake of negotiating. Every liberal political movement needs to transcend the immediate conflict by affirming larger values. The idea of a universal Good that had to be extended to the whole world was from that standpoint a blessing for all those brave American idealists, delighted with their beneficent activities in Europe, and still more in Japan, in the early fifties. But there is no crueler trap than generosity: once it became a prominent modern democracy, Japan no longer needed anyone's help and even turned into a dangerous competitor. American unionists never got over it. Of course, the unions continue to play an important role in the life of the country, but they now look conservative. The liberals have lost their faith in the unions and, after vainly pinning their hopes on one warhorse after another, are having a hard time rediscovering their identity. The vital movement of that era, as completely real and alive as it was, rested nonetheless on an illusion.

The first time I felt this disenchantment was when I interviewed Hubert Humphrey, who was already someone of importance in 1948. Still very young, the coming man of the pro-union liberals was mayor of Minneapolis. Minnesota was a bustling, politically active state, leaning rather left as a result of the strong social-democratic, populist influence of the Scandinavians and other northern Europeans. Humphrey, the son of a druggist, had been a brilliant university student and an assistant professor of political science, and had gone on to win election on the Democratic ticket. He was a union man, and in particular a UAW man, the most liberal, perhaps, of all the possible liberals.

What was striking about him was his irrepressible flow of talk. He had an answer for everything and gave you the solution even before you posed the problem. And those solutions were always on the good side, on the side of the angels. It was also an educational

15

solution. H.H.H. was always unshakably confident in the power of education. What a marvelous fellow was he, so cheerful, so devoted, so appealing. The good American who would see matters through to the end, even the Vietnam War—although, of course, he was dragged into that by Johnson . . . and by his own crusading spirit. But all his rhetoric could only make one wonder. Since everything was so simple, why were Americans not making more progress? The educating and the speechifying had been going on for years, so why did racial discrimination persist, or mass poverty, or corruption, or the Mafia?

Corruption especially was an issue that had a direct bearing on the unions. In 1948 the racketeering that prevailed in the Teamsters Union had not yet been officially exposed but was common knowledge in the labor movement. Trying to understand the situation, I read everything I could find about that union. Unfortunately, it was all too clear. On the one hand, corruption always springs up whenever cheating is easy. Among truck drivers thefts, substitutions, accidents, and foul-ups are hard to verify, hence the endemic pillage, though neither as widespread nor as organized as among the dock workers. On the other hand, transport is a matter of life and death in business, and companies will readily pay to avoid being choked off.

Without the Teamsters, a company may find itself deprived of its raw materials or unable to deliver to its clients. Thus, nothing prevents a smart union business agent from guaranteeing his friends in the executive suite the social peace they need, in exchange for a small stipend. Even if we grant that this practice is seldom seen, there nevertheless exists a wide spectrum of more sophisticated forms of rendering mutual "favors," which do no harm at all to the rank and file: the business agent can ask and get for them good wages and decent working conditions while accumulating a modest fortune for himself. Later, when he has a little money and good friends in the right places, it's easy to make his financial garden bloom. Within a short time many of these local potentates had hundreds of thousands of dollars to play with. The commissions they received on the group health insurance contracts signed by their members often served as their seed money. Without being gangsters like the ones in Elia Kazan's film *On the Waterfront* (1954), they represented a very broad sphere of semicorruption, at the heart of which flourished some far more serious crimes.

In 1948 the leadership of the Teamsters had not yet been taken over by Jimmy Hoffa, the czar of Detroit (and later Robert Kennedy's number one enemy), who spent a number of years in prison before finally being murdered. The key man then was Dave Beck, president of the Northwest Conference of the Teamsters, who ruled over the mosaic of regional fiefs that the union was at the time. Ensconced in Seattle, Beck was the archetypal nouveau riche. Luxurious quarters, elaborate woodwork, upholstered double doors, platinum blonde secretaries, plush carpets: the boss had become a VIP. Named a Regent of the University of Washington, he was not a little proud of the title. When I went to see him, I found a fat man well over fifty but in excellent shape, fresh from his daily jog. I was vividly struck by the lecture he gave me, which was every bit as edifying as Humphrey's. He was a little less intelligent, to be sure, but quick and with pat answers for everything: less virtuous than Humphrey but with no less conviction. He was a thoroughly sincere Democrat, a supporter of Truman and the Marshall Plan, an apologist for education. His union was spending a good deal of money on organization campaigns and political action; and, although it by no means always agreed with the UAW, it likewise fought *for the good cause.* As proof of his efficiency and sincerity, he cited Teamster salaries, which were higher, on the average, than those of auto workers.

This deserves a moment's reflection, because the breakdown of the union ideal is in large part attributable to such situations. Quite apart from all the corruption, what is at issue here is obviously not so much justice as power. If the Teamsters were earning more money, the reason was that they were in a position to blackmail the rest of society, much more so than were the auto workers. The law of supply and demand, which was thought to straighten everything out in the long run, seemed to be in no hurry to intervene. Let's compare with Europe. This very common problem, so devastating to any kind of idealism, arises especially on the level of public services such as the Electricité de France, which can paralyze the entire country at a moment's notice by the flick of a switch. That explains the key position of electrical workers in the Confédération Générale du Travail and the Communist party, which derive from it a tremendous potential for influencing French society. But in France, it is a question of political power and not of selfish excess or corporate abuse. The machinery is the same, however. For that matter, American unions in 1948 were hardly innocent when it came to political manipulation. The madness of McCarthyism and the heinous witch-hunt that would ravage the American Left did not materialize out of thin air: communists and fellow travelers were, in fact, in plentiful supply and played a hefty role, especially in the unions. Here the problem was the obverse of corruption. Sooner or later every organizer or business agent has to face some strong temptations, and the lofty moral stan-

17

dard that used to be invoked in labor's early days is by itself seldom enough to fight them off. The only recourse, then, is to ideology, which, just like corruption, deflects the labor movement from its true direction: it attempts to lead people away from the path they first wanted to take. This was "for their own good," of course, with no intention of reaping any other advantage than influencing immediate events and, in a broader sense, the course of history. But that is no trifling matter.

In this way a fair number of middle-level union leaders, having infiltrated key positions, secretly worked for the cause of communism. And the workers, who were often served a daily diet of Soviet propaganda from breakfast on, after listening to the news, regularly voted for those officials in company elections, because they were more zealous, honest, and efficient than the others. When the rumors started to fly, they refused to believe it: communism was the supreme evil, and no one as upstanding as Joe Blow could be in the service of evil. It should be added, by the way, that these "revolutionaries" could do little except devote themselves with greater energy than the others to union activities and wait for better days. The labor movement made the most of their devotion, which could not be put off by any job, however onerous. When they were thrown out, the unions suffered. Virtue alone was not sufficient to protect the labor people from temptation; even the UAW soon witnessed the installation of an ordinary bureaucratic machine.

The Nature of the Illusion

Thirty-five years later, the idea of a labor party on the English style as union activists imagined it, seems incongruous, even absurd. The intellectuals have deserted the unions, which they view as profoundly conservative organizations. The broad dissemination of new Marxian scriptures throughout the universities undoubtedly preserves the magical aura that still clings to the phrase "working class." But in reality those words now designate blacks, women, homosexuals, and the Third World, anything but the unions. The political roadblock set up by the southern Democrats was taken down during the Johnson presidency, without anyone's noticing it. This transformation, which the Left had so long and passionately hoped for, has not had any of the expected results. Not only has conservatism not given ground but it has spread all over the country. The worst racial problems are now in the North.

The unions themselves have lost much of their vitality. The

Teamsters have yet to be really cleaned up. The UAW has been losing out to the craft unions. George Meany, the conservative head of the AFL–CIO and principal spokesman for the corporative craft ideology, survived by more than fifteen years his younger colleague Walter Reuther, whose death in a plane crash in 1970 was a painful loss. The fruitless annual campaigns to unionize the southern textile industry go on. The UAW, moreover, bureaucratized and weighted down by the system of collective contracts, is forced to direct its main efforts toward saving jobs at Chrysler and the other automakers. Beyond these simple facts, one notes that the weakening of the unions, their lessening economic, social, and political influence owes largely to the decrease of the working class population and particularly of industrial blue-collar workers, who make up the unions' traditional clientele.

But why, one may ask, haven't the unions succeeded in organizing the white-collar workers, the people employed in offices, hospitals, and the service industries? The reason is that American unionism by its very nature relies on the model of free negotiation, and, despite appearances, it always favors minorities: the ones who gain the most from such negotiations are not the big battalions but the small, well-organized groups who can practice the most effective kind of extortion at the right moment. So it isn't necessary or even useful to waste time trying to unionize the world. What the unions did in the years from 1935 to 1950 was made possible by the Great Depression, which provoked an outburst of idealism. And even then the labor movement in its classic form, as represented by the AFL, did little to unionize the leading industries.

Today the unions cluster together well-established minorities, which profit from their situation in exactly the same way as European traditional corporations. It is no surprise that in this game the petty AFL principalities win out over the mighty union empires like those in the auto or steel industry. Nor is it any wonder if this privileged class which is often quite aware of its privileged status, should become conservative and adopt reactionary habits. The United States has only twenty million union members, usually very well paid blue-collar workers. There may be as many nonunionized white- and blue-collar workers who are also reasonably well paid. But on the other side of the fence there may be many more people who have to take home much less money: those in the lower paid service jobs, those working at the numerous odd jobs a complex society requires, and also the great cohort of people on some sort of welfare. Then finally the illegal immigrants working off the books whose number could vary according to the experts consulted from three to twelve million and who often receive starvation wages. If you add up people on welfare and illegal immigrants you get a figure much higher than the total union members.

The end of the sixties witnessed a backlash by the hardhats. With their excellent incomes, construction workers are a privileged middle class within the middle class of union members. They feel that their position is threatened by disorder and insecurity and by the promotion into their ranks of blacks and other minorities. The neighborhoods where they live are becoming the prime scene of concern over street crime and deteriorating public services. They own their own homes and cannot easily move elsewhere. Furthermore, property taxes have been rising to pay for welfare, they say, with some emphasis. Their schools, threatened by the minorities, are getting worse and worse, and the future looks dim for their children, who are having an increasingly hard time getting scholarships preferentially awarded to minorities. If reactionary candidates give special attention to working class neighborhoods, it is not without cause or success.

The major industries appear to be on the downslide, which situation England knows so well. By constantly asking for more, in the best tradition of Samuel Gompers, American union representatives have locked themselves into a no-win situation. Contrary to what they think, technical progress has not kept up with their demands and contractual gains. The incredible proliferation of the legal bureaucracy built up to administer collective agreements has not spurred innovation but curbed it. The major American industries are no longer up to date, either technologically or socially. And the standard of living of American workers has begun to fall. The idea of social progress through free negotiation has long since reached its limits. Far from having some universal value, it worked only in a climate of general expansion. When the frontier vanishes, when the age of the finite world begins, institutional mechanisms throw themselves into reverse, and what was once the source of progress threatens to lead to decline.

CHAPTER TWO

UNIVERSITY AMERICA

or

the Dream of Truth

The Dream of Truth

P EOPLE NEVER ABANDON a dream simply because they can no longer believe in it. They develop it, enlarge it, transform it, until one day they notice that it has become a different dream. The dream of the American Left was to lay hold of social progress through combat that might be radical or even violent, but unburdened by useless intellectual baggage and untainted by revolutionary excesses. In 1948, long before Cuba or even Yugoslavia came into vogue among the European Left, the United States was the home of that dream. I was a pro-American leftist, a somewhat rare species in France, but one that still could be respectable. To be treated well, I had to be called an independent Marxist. It was a generous position, it did not compromise with either the Right or the Left, and above all it was concrete. But dreams of this sort shrivel up unless their vigor is continually renewed. And American unionism was barely advancing. The ideal was getting bogged down in routine, sinking into a legal quagmire. But I felt no disappointment: the fact was that for the moment I had not noticed anything. It would take years before I was capable of challenging my illusions from that era.

In the fifties an America, which I had almost completely ignored during my earlier trip, came imperceptibly to take the place of the first. This one was intellectual America, which also had a dream—the dream of truth. It was very attractive for anyone who had decided to study society. For the most part, naturally, interest in this sort of study derives never from a simple taste for knowledge as such but rather from the hope of changing things. One wants to do one's share in building a new world, and not by handing out leaflets (either because one thinks that is not enough or cannot believe what the leaflets say). Nonetheless, when this hope has been dashed, one is quite willing to replace it with the love of knowledge and to reinvest one's expectations in the idea of truth.

To understand the force of this second dream, it is necessary to recall what French society, and all of Europe except the United Kingdom, were like in those days: countries torn apart and trampled under, rejecting their old culture but without managing to go beyond it. Those who came of age in the fifties were totally paralyzed by the frantic rhetoric of the grand masters who ruled the world of ideology and whose revolutionary veneer barely hid their aristocratic arrogance. Intellectual America, by contrast, was every bit as generous as working class America. A foreigner might have thought himself transported back to the time of the French Revolution, with the famous sign marking the border, "Here begins the land of Liberty." This time it would be the land of truth. In the university neither race nor color nor religion nor ideology had the slightest importance. The grand army of scientists was open to whoever came to serve the cause of Truth, with the sole stipulation that the norms of scientific work be respected and the rule that no statement be accepted without proof. No other preconditions or hidden requirements: a cat is a cat, even in Patagonian, and if that does not hold for the language of Marxism-Leninism, then that language is useless. Too bad, the scientist would have said without the least trace of irony, it looked interesting.

Most of the classroom chairs at Harvard University are alike; austere design, black lacquer finish, and marked with the university's emblem: a gilded tripartite coat of arms stamped with Gothic letters: VE-RI-TAS. I was often tempted to steal some of those emblems, but I could never bring myself to do so. After all, you cannot simply appropriate the Truth. How wonderful, it seemed to me, that participants in an intellectual discussion should have to sit on *Veritas* chairs. One knows what one is there for, that one has to hear the other man out and move ahead with him, that the idea is not to wrangle or to try to get the upper hand but to cooperate in the labor of truth.

In France they then had no respect for the truth. Besides, it did not exist; it was a bourgeois invention. Before you did anything else you had to define from what standpoint you were talking; you had to demonstrate the correctness of this position and the purity of your soul. It was not like that in America. It made little difference, as far as truth was concerned, whether you were white or yellow, a Marxist or a positivist. The most respected people in your field listened to you without hesitation. They invited you to their offices not to dazzle you or to perform for you, as European academics would have done, but in the hope that you would have something to teach them. And, in fact, thanks to their ability to listen, they succeeded in retrieving some fragment of truth from your desultory remarks. "Young man, don't forget that this is the land of Truth": I was finding my old Washington mentor again, but I had never actually lost him: it was, after all, the same values and the same country.

This truth that American intellectuals glorified owed much of its appeal to its concrete, practical character. I heard them say repeatedly, with an epicurean smile, "There's nothing more practical than a good theory." And if truth served as the object of a cult celebrated in the universities and research centers, its rites had an austerity not at all marred by a sort of fastidious simplicity: say what you have to say, but say it quickly. Any true theory can hold up on the strength of a phrase and three equations, even in the social sciences. The rest is just wordy preface, useless formality, digression, and decadent European flourish. I could never conform totally to this discipline. I was too concerned with nuances; I felt the need to spell out the context and the limits of validity of what I had to say. But nowhere did I learn more.

Later on, to be sure, I often saw my models turn pompous or play the prima donna like the Europeans. Since then, fortunately, Europe has changed, and America even more, so the two worlds have come much closer together. Still, I shall never forget America in its role as the Land of Truth, a naive land perhaps, but grand and generous. It was good for all humanity, even crucial, that one country knew how to keep that passion burning with such intensity when all the others had wavered.

Austere Michigan

The cult of truth was probably nowhere so well nurtured, at least as far as the human sciences go, as in the educational institutions of the austere state of Michigan. Austerity fits the landscape of plains and

lakes, with only pines and birches and pale sunlight. The home of
the automobile industry, that gigantic, monstrous, monomaniacal
business, is also the home of austere intellectuals—careful, earnest
people, a bit like Scandinavian Illuminati. Michigan is the state with
the highest per capita outlay for its public universities, of which the
best is the University of Michigan at Ann Arbor, not far from Detroit.
When I went there to visit for the first time in 1956, the city had just
elected as its mayor a professor of political science from the university.
Scholarship was held in such high esteem that some of the more liberal
executives in the auto industry had forsaken exclusive Grosse Pointe
to live in Ann Arbor. Robert S. McNamara was one of them: only an
act of God could make him miss a major academic cocktail party. A
number of UAW officials showed like enthusiasm. Little by little the
university was civilizing the crude ways of the big city.

For my part, I came to Ann Arbor in connection with one of the
"productivity missions" which the Marshall Plan had imposed on the
Europeans and which made a key contribution toward the transformation of Europe. When agreements for the Plan were signed, the
Americans demanded that a large portion of the credits provided be
devoted to research and the training of European elites. So productivity missions were organized, which allowed hundreds of Europeans
from the most varied fields to spend several weeks in the United States,
during which they were shown the latest advances in their specialty:
how things were done, and why.

There was a lot to see in a limited time, and most of the pilgrims
came away exhausted. But this crash program proved to be extraordinarily effective. And this period marks the beginning of the hunger
for information, the study trips, the professional discussions, in a
word, the open-mindedness that characterizes economic and social
activities in Europe today—to the degree that in this respect the Europeans are often ahead of the Americans. Up until this program
they would conceal jealously their experiences and their secrets, but
this discovery of America radically transformed them. They learned
that it was possible to talk and discuss these matters. The Europeans
caught the virus of progress, which they still have not shaken. France,
for example, has built an entire industry of continuing education;
French executives have become addicts of seminar training. None of
it would have been conceivable without this initial "contamination."

Michigan was the goal of our pilgrimage. We members of the
productivity mission spent a week there, without a moment to catch
our breath, listening to the most important researchers in social psychology as they took stock of their area of expertise and presented

their hypotheses and findings. I have never learned so many things in so short a time. In the fifties their great problem, and mine, was hierarchical relationships. All their liberal, optimistic theories revolved around the notion of permissiveness. They tried to demonstrate that permissive methods of authority could not only be more satisfying but also more efficient than authoritarian methods. They worked in the laboratory conducting experimental research on volunteers— mostly students, of course—and attempted to verify their models and hypotheses through extensive studies of business and government. But they never spanned the gap between their methodology and the real world, apart from a few inconclusive and abortive efforts. Yet in those days they still had high hopes of getting there, sooner or later.

Whereas in other research centers there was excited talk about an imminent methodological breakthrough, at Ann Arbor the researchers insisted above all on scientific accuracy. I recall one researcher who explained to us that his results had completely undermined his hypotheses, but who saw in this a remarkable success, because he had managed to eliminate the "null hypothesis"—that plague of the approximative social sciences, which strikes when an operational model designed to produce a clear black and white picture generates instead (as it most often does) a gray blotch. In this instance the investigator got pure black—in other words, he had clearly been wrong. His findings disproved the liberal, optimistic theory on which he had based his research. But, putting Truth far ahead of his personal desires, he was that much more exultant. His self-refutation testified to the quality of his work. The God of Truth demanded sacrifices, and the more costly they were, the stronger the devotee's faith became.

On the whole, however, these academics still passionately believed that permissiveness was destined to infuse new life into humanity and society. Many other universities and research centers were doing work inspired by the same premises. All America was caught up in a powerful, quasi-religious movement, which in its various manifestations, from Dr. Benjamin Spock to encounter groups, has had a deeply unsettling effect on Western societies. But it was in Michigan that a respected scientific laboratory first embarked on this adventure. Treat your neighbor well, and he will treat you well. Rather than punishing your subordinates for their shortcomings, take an interest in their problems: they will like you more for it, and as a bonus you will get a jump in productivity. The idea was to show how "virtuous" circles could counter the vicious ones of aggression and the pecking order.

The notion was simplistic, because there is no responsible way of defining either the conditions under which virtue can single-handedly maintain itself or the means to be used for moving from a destructive to a beneficial spiral. Still, many different ideas, both good and bad, emerged from such thinking: the illusions about human relations and public relations that threw the European Left off course in the fifties; the illusions of social psychology; much of the libertarian dream of the students revolutionary movement; the glorification of personal encounter; the challenge hurled at institutions; the disorder rampant in the educational system.[1]

In the Land of the Think Tanks

The best example I know of an institution based on the idea of a "virtuous circle" comes from this very same world of research. If the research institute connected with the University of Michigan followed an ethic and a mode of operation conceived very much along academic lines, America had also discovered in the fifties an altogether new approach: the think tank. The recipe was simple: find a large enough supply of proven intellectuals and promising young people, throw them together, free them from all constraints—administrative, technical and, as far as possible, social—pay them handsomely, send them off on stimulating projects, then simply let them think and see what happens.

The think tanks were developed after the pattern of the Princeton Institute for Advanced Study, where Einstein had been the shining star, and to some extent the more mundane Brookings Institution in Washington.

The most successful of these institutions during the fifties and sixties was the Rand Corporation, where Herman Kahn began his career, and by "thinking the unthinkable" became a legend in his own time.

The extraordinary aspect of the think tank phenomenon is the immense prestige it suddenly bestows on the simple *act* of thinking. Needless to say, the world had not waited for the Americans to arrive before admiring knowledge and even wisdom. But I was struck by this American phenomenon. Their respect was raised to the nth degree, and everything conspired to create ideal conditions where the thoughts of a handful of chosen individuals can take off in any direction. Each of them, alone in his monkish room, far from the both-

[1]Far be it from me to trace all this back to one intellectual discovery, and to make Michigan the hothouse for the modern world in the sixties. It is nonetheless interesting to see the connections of its scientific hypotheses with some of the basic issues of the sociopolitical debate of the time.

ersome details of the lab and the 101 classroom chores, performs his devotions at a pristine blackboard. The atmosphere around him is ideally suited to reflection: warm, supportive, but totally silent. There are no telephones or discussions in the corridors. Like the "Quiet, we're shooting" barked out on the soundstage, a cry seems to echo down the halls here, "Quiet, he's thinking." Somehow, it was impossible to visualize this in a French setting.

In 1959–60 I was a resident in one such think tank, the Center for Advanced Study in the Behavioral Sciences at Stanford. This center followed the Princeton model very closely. Each September it took in forty-five persons for one year only. On a site facing the rolling hills that overlook Stanford University, each fellow occupied a private bungalow furnished with bookshelves and the inevitable blackboard. Every morning someone came to ask what books he wanted fetched from the university library. The center had not been in existence for more than five years and, though well on its way, it was still buoyed up by high enthusiasm. That year turned out to be a year of individualism, and group projects were not too popular. As if to make up for that, there was much hobnobbing from bungalow to bungalow, people conferred, exchanged first drafts, held discussions out in the sun in the relaxed mood of picnic lunches.

The center had been created by the Ford Foundation to strengthen university research in the behavioral sciences, a field in which the foundation played a crucial role in the fifties and sixties. It was explained to me that behavioral sciences meant human sciences but from a perspective sharply positivistic-concrete, intent on empirical proof, oriented toward experimentation and the analysis of possible practical consequences. The overriding concern of the Ford Foundation was the so-called cultural lag separating the human sciences from technology and the natural sciences, which were going full steam ahead, knocking human behavioral patterns and social codes topsy-turvy. This challenge had to be set to prevent runaway innovation hence the need for investing in the behavioral sciences. The logic was impeccable, and the Ford Foundation pressed it to the limit.

Here again, American efficiency was remarkable. Everything was carefully attended to, down to the last detail. The selection of each year's fellows was made through an intricate system of elitist democracy. To be sure of getting the best candidates, the foundation circulated lists of applicants to the outstanding figures in each discipline. Then it did its best to draw up a balanced roster, factoring in age, area of study, and particular orientation. The final choices, once arrived at, were immune to question: Ford seemed always to be satisfied in its selection of candidates. Apart from a ban on music and sports on the premises, the chosen fellows would know no other rule for a year than Rabelais's generous maxim, "Do what you will."

Civilized Students

For an academic, the path I followed in the United States was somewhat irregular: first unions, then research institutes, then think tanks, and only then university teaching. In 1967, without prior teaching experience, without ever having been a student in the United States, I was called upon to teach at Harvard. Each stage had been a new shock: liberal America, so open and dynamic, jolted a timid student arriving from bureaucratic French society; rigorous research jolted a young European intellectual more accustomed to abstract generalities; the absolute freedom of Stanford jolted a mind brought up to respect form and hierarchy. And finally the honor bestowed upon me by Harvard caught me just as unaware. I had never taught, not even in France, but I was to hold the rank of full professor in the most prestigious university in the United States. Everywhere else in America, it seemed, including excellent universities such as Berkeley or Michigan, many people still had a considerable sense of cultural distance from the world "back east." There they have "class," they would say they are less naive, they represent civilization itself. Especially at Harvard.

And then one day I found those civilized students sitting before me—a good hundred of them—more than I had been led to expect. I panicked a little, garbled my lines, went on too long. At the second meeting there were no more than forty, at the third, twenty-five. It was no use telling myself that a small class was better than a thronged amphitheater; I still felt mortified. A whole week went by before I discovered that there was nothing peculiar about these defections, that I had shared the common lot of all professors: the students were simply shopping around. Nobody holds onto his initial audience. Twenty-five persons for your first course, they told me, you should be happy, that's a success.

Those twenty-five faithful, in any case, were wonderfully cooperative. I was not always perfectly intelligible, both from nervousness and the language problem. When the students could not follow me, they made me repeat what I had said, without the least embarrassment but always graciously. And if I continued to be vague on this point or that, they generously put it down to my English, never to any imprecision in my thinking, which they helped me to clarify. The course was taught with, rather than to, them, and the more I called upon them to contribute, the better they liked it.

What a difference between this and France! They were not there to criticize or yawn their way through the hour, but to make the most of an opportunity they had been offered. That was immediately evident from the extraordinary capacity these young men and women had for listening—nothing I said got past them. The simple fact of their attention loosened my tongue, and when the words did not come or were not clear, they encouraged me by their questions. These led to more personal exchanges, which were almost always fruitful. "You say that," a student would venture, "and it's a fascinating idea, but couldn't you also say that . . ." Or, "Your analysis makes me think of . . ." If I answered, "No, I don't see the connection," he was not in the least offended. And thanks to his interest I could take off from there, extracting from a somewhat naive question the awkwardly expressed intuition it almost always contained: "The way you put it, the argument doesn't hold, but you've got your finger on something essential here, which might bring up another interesting interpretation. . . ." Here too we were moving in a "virtuous spiral," and we worked together in an altogether remarkable fashion. All the more so because—a bolt from the blue for a French instructor—I could suggest that they read such and such a book, and they would read it. Even better, they would read it in time for us to have some serious conversation about it.

They were, in fact, truly civilized students. Strongly independent, they showed no sign of obsequiousness, but acted with a natural deference, full of geniality and human warmth. When I think of the two semesters of teaching I did back then, I am tempted to say that whoever has not known the better American universities in the sixties has not known the joy of teaching. My students enriched me in many ways; they even influenced my research work. Without them I would never have managed to expand my vision of bureaucracy, which was narrowly confined to France. I presented to them the French cases I had studied, along with my analysis of their inner mechanisms, forcefully repeating—as a precaution but also by a kind of reverse chauvinism—that all of it was specifically French, that only France could produce such monstrous results.

The students were more than willing to accept my method of research and my line of reasoning with the hypotheses it was based on, but only on condition that they could extend them beyond the context of France. My propositions struck them as useful, so they ought to hold for the United States as well. And, as a matter of fact, after working on their own, studying concrete cases, and writing term papers about them, they convinced me that on this point I was wrong, that despite Philip the Fair and Louis XIV, bureaucracy was no more peculiarly French than it was peculiarly American. From then on I could never talk about administration and bureaucracy, in France or elsewhere, as I had before.

An Aftertaste of Sadness

In 1980, I went back to teach at Harvard. On the surface the students were the same as ever—quick, open, intelligent, hard working. But they were sad, they had no appetite for anything; the future looked to them to be a dead end. To be sure, French students are also sad, but then they have always grumbled, fumed, and protested, without either themselves or anybody else attaching much importance to it. Everyone knows too well that after all this noble dissent, he will ultimately figure out a scheme for making his peace with a rotten world. But sad Americans are another story: their sorrow is uncomplicated, unrelenting, uninflected. To stir them up a little I had to provoke them, telling them bluntly that their future depended in the first instance upon themselves, that in a country like theirs intellectuals would never want for work, that there would be room for people capable of fighting.

Here I could make some contact with them. But if I waited for them to spontaneously reach out to me, nothing happened. Born too late in a world grown old, they had lost heart. This feeling, moreover, went beyond simple indifference or apathy. I could sense in it a derisive flavor, almost a delight in failure. In my graduate seminar I asked for examples of American social innovations whose patterns of emergence and development we could examine together. Half the suggestions I got concerned reprehensible innovations, advances in evil. The first student to volunteer wanted to study ABSCAM, the FBI's latest weapon in the war against corruption. Why not, my student asked, it's a new tactic, dishonest, certainly, but new. And we should look at the bad innovations, too—they could be more important than the good ones.

No more than I would claim that all American women are redheads, I would not go so far as to argue that American students, after seeing nothing but good for years, are now incapable of seeing anything but evil. But there *is* obviously a discouraging wind blowing. And a perverse reaction is impelling young Americans to burn what

America once adored, to trample its positive idols, to take a jaundiced view of everything.

This mood shift can be seen even in the research going on in the social sciences. The machine continues to grind away; myriad projects still get their funding, but people are entirely engulfed in what Thomas Kuhn (in *The Structure of Scientific Revolutions*) calls "normal science," the daily professional routine.[2] Such work provides an ever-increasing degree of rigor and precision—on decreasingly interesting subjects, along with statistics, more statistics, and interminable footnotes. The work is careful, but imagination is atrophying.

And when studies do leave this beaten track, the propositions they assert and the experiences they describe betray once again a deep fascination with evil. The success of Stanley Milgram's *Obedience to Authority* is, from this standpoint, particularly impressive: his experiments run almost diametrically counter to those conducted in Michigan some twenty years ago.[3] Back then the idea was to show that the right kind of permissiveness would produce both deeper satisfaction for the people directly affected by it and better results for the whole group. Milgram by contrast strives to prove that by manipulating various elements in a given social context, one can transform any ordinary peaceful citizen into a Nazi torturer.

Virtuous spiral, vicious spirals: it would be interesting to show that both spirals can function in the real world, depending on the situation, and to try to understand how the transition from one to the other occurs, what triggers a shift to the right or wrong direction. Whatever one thinks of the (debatable) scientific significance of Milgram's experiments, the essential point is that their success rests on the larger intention that inspired them—just as the success of the permissive ideology had little to do with the quality of the theories that the Michigan experiments were designed to establish. America has undoubtedly believed too long and too ardently in the good, thus paving the way for this deplorable turnaround.

Naturally, this is only one aspect of the situation. During these same months as a teacher in America I met a number of young graduates of French professional schools, licensed engineers,[4] who saw

[2]Thomas S. Kuhn, *The Structure of Scientific Revolutions* (Chicago: University of Chicago Press, 1962).

[3]Stanley Milgram, *Obedience to Authority* (New York: Harper & Row, 1974).

[4]It is now de rigueur for members of the French elite to spend a postgraduate year at MIT, Berkeley, or Harvard. Among European students in the United States the French are often the largest and most active group.

things quite differently. They were amazed at the freedom of thought, the practical sense, and the confidence in people that still permeate American university life. Having just left behind a France they called "bastardly," they felt blissfully at home in America, and in their philosophical moments they played their own variations on the everlasting theme of comparing the two countries to the detriment of France. Clearly they were not wrong, but paradoxically one look at them was convincing evidence that France, too, had changed: with their high-spirited, go-getter style, they were more American than the Americans. They were the ones who were rushing off to win the West, while many of their American comrades had given up and were putting one foot in front of the other strictly out of habit.

Fifteen years ago I knew many happy American intellectuals with happy families. The world lay spread before them, people came to consult them, their words carried weight in the community. The universities were cathedrals for the worship of triumphant rationality. Some businessmen, I was told, would eventually commute by plane to audit classes given by a famous professor. The children of these intellectuals were all exceptionally gifted, guaranteed to have brilliant futures. If the nascent postindustrial society was in the process of creating a ruling class, this could only be the "theory class," so dear to a pair of sociologists as well informed (and mutually incompatible) as Daniel Bell and John Kenneth Galbraith.

But the triumphalism misfired, and within a few years the happy intellectuals had turned bitter. Their young prodigies came to grief from drugs, or they became carpenters. Courses in theory are still being given, at Harvard and elsewhere, but nobody flies in any more to take them. The students are blasé, and the professors are tired. The privileged experts who once knowingly calculated the chances other societies had of achieving an American level of efficiency and social consensus are now in turn stricken with a morbid sense of powerlessness and doubt. Can it be that the achievements of a civilization come and go, like fashion or economic cycles?

Of course, hindsight can supply economic and sociological explanations for this collapse of a university system, if one has failed to analyze its inner workings when there was still time. This system functioned in an expansionary mode: competition was good because there was room for everybody. In order to succeed, a professor had to publish his work as fast as possible, so as to make a name for himself and to attract the best students. The latter would contribute to his success, because good students make for good research. The value of the researcher would be enhanced; he would enjoy all the more recognition as his disciples made his ideas bear fruit and became important in their own right.

That is why it paid not to hide away while preparing the stunning announcement of results secretly accumulated over the years, which is the European system, but on the contrary to practice a policy of openness, generosity, and, in a word, *expansion*. A scientist or scholar of established reputation would take under his wing four or five brilliant doctoral students to help him carry out his research program. Herein lay the crux of the problem; programs lasted for only three or four years. And the bright new Ph.D.'s whose dissertations had been invariably all first rate would have to find a place in the system. They would require, each of them the financing of their own research programs for which they would surround themselves with four or five young lions, still more brilliant and with still sharper teeth. Even allowing for some inevitable setbacks, this arrangement necessarily led to a much too rapid geometrical increase of scientists and scholars, a process that sooner or later had to come to a crashing stop: at that rate within fifty years half the population of America would have been involved in research.

Nevertheless, this expansion went on for a rather long time, from 1950 to 1970, because means were available for supporting a large number of scientists, and because the baby boom and the spread of higher education created new jobs. New universities sprang up, the state universities expanded, small rural colleges in a few years developed into large, prosperous institutions with hundreds of faculty posts to offer. The freedom to recruit, in this well-oiled competitive system, accelerated the process: the newer universities, especially in California, outbid the others for the services of academic stars, and by raising salary levels increased the attractiveness, for the best students, of prestigious careers, which could be made even more lucrative by serving as a consultant or working part time for research and development companies. And the funds for research, like the needs of industry and the state, seemed infinite. All progressive minds throughout the world admired such a system and wanted it to be emulated in their own countries.

Around the end of the sixties, however, this educational boom began to have some absurd consequences. In 1970 the market first went bearish for physics, the pace-setting science, which had drawn the most brilliant students. The physicists, suddenly finding themselves superfluous, fell back upon cognate fields, thereby creating a chain reaction in all the exact sciences and ultimately affecting even the social sciences. At almost the same time a crisis broke out in the humanities. There the rate of growth had not been so hectic, but the abrupt halt of university expansion also had a dramatic effect on their job market.

The happy upward spiral of the recent past reversed itself in an alarmingly downward vicious circle. The most talented students betook themselves to the professions, to business, law, or medical schools—the only schools that could assure the future of their graduates. (Programs are even set up now for the rapid retooling of brand new Ph.D.'s in literature and the social sciences for careers in management.) The most gifted young people are no longer drawn to research, and those already engaged in it have lost the old feeling of excitement. The mandarins have retired to their ivory towers, assistantships are filled by increasingly mediocre candidates. As a result, research has become less creative and attracts fewer financial backers. Dwindling funds are serving to strengthen the forces already driving the most promising minds away from academia, and so on and on it goes in an accelerating downward spiral.

Clearly, we cannot talk about the crisis in American universities without acknowledging the importance of these basic mechanisms. Still, if this explanation told the whole story, it surely would have been possible to mitigate the violence of the crisis and above all to maintain the energy level of the most gifted and dedicated academics. But, as fate would have it, around that very same time an altogether different moral crisis was wrenching the entire country and in particular its intellectual elite: agony over the Vietnam War. This is the reason the jamming of the apparatus of supply and demand produced such drastic effects. In addition, the nationwide crisis made it practically impossible to face the difficulties in a rational spirit. When scientists have stopped believing in science and social scientists care only about protest, there is no hope of their getting the engine started again. And since their negative attitude was hardly attractive to benefactors, grants and research money began to dry up just when they were needed most.

The Illusion of Righteousness

But we must dig still deeper: if the system experienced so grave a moral crisis owing to economic problems and the Vietnam tragedy, some intrinsic weakness undoubtedly prevented it from overcoming obstacles and adapting to the situation. The aftertaste of sadness that I sensed so strongly in 1980 was something I had already perceived in May 1970 at the end of my last teaching session. It had been a

good year for my students and myself, despite the unrest over Vietnam and the university antiwar strikes. My students were full of enthusiasm as they fought against the war, for justice, for all of humanity.
The problems on their conscience were simple ones, and they did not
resent having a European like me try to temper their certitudes with
a bit of skepticism.

Then, after the bombing in Cambodia, came the last rumbling
wave of disturbances: demonstrations, sit-ins, protests of various sorts
all across the country. At the beginning of May the shootings occurred
at Kent State University. On a campus in the heart of one of those
Midwest reactionary states some National Guardsmen, believing themselves outflanked by demonstrators, were ordered by their officers to
open fire. The unarmed crowd pressing forward, the soldiers firing
into their midst: it was a replay of the classic revolutionary scene. But
here it had a touch of the grotesque, because the Ohio National Guard
was made up not of mercenary soldiers but of decent people from
around the corner—grocers, plumbers, gas station attendants, panic-
stricken by a situation that was completely over their heads. And the
crowd held no proletarian insurgents in battle formation, nor even
any sophisticated young ideologues who had read Marx in the original,
but the children of these same grocers, plumbers, and gas station
attendants, belatedly joining the rest of American students in their
awareness of what was going on in Vietnam.

The strike called at Harvard did not disrupt classes very much,
since the courses were ending anyhow. I proposed to my students that
we meet one more time. Just about all of them agreed, explaining,
almost by way of justification, that they had nothing better to do since,
in any case, there was nothing *to* do.

Our class discussion, naturally, revolved around the only possible
subject: the war. They were so disheartened that all of a sudden they
broke into tears, both boys and girls. It came as a shock to me, and
I realized sadly that the student antiwar movement had collapsed.
They would go no farther. This same aftertaste of sadness is what I
recognized years later. Their frustration made sense, of course: after
all, what could they have done? The situation was a dead end in all
directions.

But the underlying problem lay elsewhere: the very meaning of
everything they had done up till then was suddenly being called into
question. What had they all been hoping for? For the walls to come
tumbling down once they had gone around them seven times, proclaiming that right was on their side? Something like that happened
earlier when "the children's crusade" had caused Johnson not to run

for reelection. But for all that, the war had not stopped. When it eventually did, it would be because its momentum was exhausted, not because of anything they had done directly.

In the final analysis, the illusion exposed here was none other than the old idea so long cherished by the most traditional and peaceful elements of the American Left: the absolute confidence in justice, in equity, which necessarily had to triumph, the idea that it was enough to stand up and speak out, because there was no limit to progress. Belief in the good cause sweeps away complications: if the war is a good one, you have to go all the way and win it; if it is bad, it is totally bad and you have to drop your rifle on the spot. This is how two Americas could have a head-on collision with each side feeling equally righteous because it is, deep down, exactly the same kind of easy, too easy righteousness.

The complaint will be raised that this interpretation may shed some light on the problems of the student movement but none at all on those of the university system and of scientific research. But in reality science itself can be strongly affected by such moral issues, because science, all things considered, is not just science but a whole human system on the move. And for that movement to continue, the human system has to be inspired by a sufficiently strong faith in the possibility of development and progress. The postulate of a universal good is equally useful to scientific work. When it breaks down, scientists, too, even those in the most abstract disciplines, lose confidence, and the quality of their work suffers enormously.

This conclusion can, I think, be carried still farther. The postulate of goodness and of indefinite expansion does not stimulate the imagination long enough, nor does it promote renewal. It is no accident that American science has leaned so heavily on European scientists: Europe formed well-tempered minds, to whom America basically gave more opportunities for elaborating their ideas and who inspired serious followers. The successful record of this symbiosis must not obscure the fact that its limits are always near: when the source dries up, the system has a hard time renewing itself. This point has not been reached yet, fortunately, but we can already see the damage done by a too rapid cycle of expansion and immediate applications. The enormous machine is becoming less imaginative, and to the extent that it increases its efficiency in the short term, it will be less productive in the long term. The social sciences in particular are afflicted with this kind of deterioration, which must be taken as a danger signal for the American university system in its entirety.

In the sixties the writing was already on the wall. People had surrendered too readily to idealistic faith in the good, to the naive model of consensus and of universal education. The United States made a brave show of being a perfectly balanced society, safe from the whirling tides and dramatic conflicts of history. It was something utterly different from a Teilhardian Omega Point or a Marxist paradise but it had some of their utopian qualities.

Within this perspective American thinking on the "developing" countries was chiefly concerned with the possibilities of a gradual transition from an underdeveloped to a developed economy—W. W. Rostow's famous "take-off." Applying this notion to politics, social scientists drew up a table of all the possible combinations of variables, and then wondered how to progress from the nether regions on the graph to the ideal high point, where all the parameters were positive: the point the United States had already reached. I am caricaturing, but not that much, the naiveté typical of studies done back then. Intellectual America in those halcyon days was also a self-satisfied America, which thought it had found the key to unlimited progress and so had stopped searching. It held its truths to be absolutes, forgetting that no one truth is ever complete and that a partial truth embraced for too long becomes an insane idea.

CHAPTER THREE

DECISION-MAKING AMERICA

or
the Dream of Rationality

**The Dream of
Rationality**

THE DREAM OF TRUTH IS AS dangerous as it is necessary. Were it not for the illusion of being able to attain the truth, man would never fight for a better world. But it is a short step from this illusion to that of possessing the truth, which opens the door to the worst aberrations. Thanks to more solid values perhaps one day humanity will manage to stay away from that temptation, to keep the sacred fire alive without burning down the temple. Let us hope so. But the illusion of rationality is more dangerous, and by its very nature prevents its victims from coming to their senses, because it involves believing in the possibility of placing a second bet with money not yet won from an earlier bet. Starting out with a single, and always uncertain, truth, one deduces "a long interlocking series of perfectly simple and natural reasons." The end result will most probably be an imposing figure with feet of clay.

Nevertheless, the idea of rationality is just as indispensable as the dream of truth. We absolutely must believe not only that two and two are four but that a good method gives better results than a bad one and that, still more generally, it is better to look ahead before leaping. Unfortunately, from these necessary beliefs people rush too easily into conclusions that verge on madness: for example, abstract formulas can be taken straight from the drawing board to reality, whatever can be well conceived and clearly expressed must be right, coherence is a good test of reliability, and so on. Refine those maxims a bit, turn them into a system, and disaster will not be far behind.

I did not immediately encounter the illusion of rationality in America during the sixties, and when I did still less did I appreciate its seriousness, shielded as I was by both the university milieu and my situation as a foreigner. I still subscribed to the cliché, so widespread among Europeans and even Americans themselves, of seeing America as above all else the land of pragmatism. In my opinion, by seeking out every possible practical application of science, Americans were merely wedding their traditional pragmatism to the more recent cult of truth, whose strictness I found powerfully attractive.

I had yet to discover that Americans, far from being more pragmatic than Europeans, are in certain ways much less so—precisely because they believe too categorically, too naively, in truth and rationality. Hence, they turn more readily into cynics than into skeptics. If the smugness and complacency of American theoreticians know no limits, it is due to their unusual faculty for losing touch with reality. When they are on stage, hubris and rhetorical excess are always in the wings. Nonetheless, I believed in this dream myself. The temptation was difficult to resist. It was so exciting, everything in America was so simple, so fast, so efficient. People got straight to the point, frankly, calmly, naturally. Ideas wasted no time in finding their embodiment in deeds, action was finally becoming twin sister to the dream.

In Paris getting three self-styled important people to have lunch together requires a clever secretary and several weeks. The lunch itself will take at least two-and-a-half hours, with half or two-thirds the time squandered on preliminaries, jockeying for position, witticisms, and idle chatter. At Harvard, luncheon dates were agreed on instantly, man to man, and never lasted more than an hour and a quarter. Ten minutes to order the food and get through the customary jokes, by way of showing that one was in good form, then at once down to business. What to talk about? I would like to put points 1, 2, and 3 on the agenda. He does not want to get into 2 right away, but would like to add 4 and 5. I agree about 5, but I'd prefer to save 4 till the end, because I first have to be clear on everything else. Having spent barely five minutes working out this program, we go to item 1. The questions are pointed, the answers precise. Here words carry weight, are pregnant with action, lead to new reflections, with no divorce between doing and thinking. If a stray intuition happens to cross your mind, you can even interrupt the exchange to make room for it: "That reminds me of . . ." You open the parenthesis for two minutes, close it, and come back to it later on. The partners in the conversation may be working together or each for himself. One of them may write in a footnote of some future paper, "I owe this idea to my friend So-and-so." The pleasures of listening, the pleasures of being listened to. You return the serve without trying to hit a winner in a splendid game of tennis where no one keeps score. You feel the joy of a mind liberated from matter; by the time you have your coffee, you're a little vague about what you ate, but is that really so important to know?

At Harvard the best exercise I had in the art of well-modulated rationality came in a seminar on the Cuban missile crisis. There were only seven or eight persons in the group. Our purpose was to arrive at a decision theory capable of integrating the various elements connected with political life, administrative processes, and all the other material contingencies that, like so many noses of Cleopatra, hinder the progress of rationality.

The basis for our work was the thesis of an extremely brilliant doctoral student, Graham Allison,[1] who was also the secretary of the group; our subject of discussion was the genesis of President John F. Kennedy's handling of the missile crisis. We were not interested in gathering the facts of the case: Allison had already done a lot of work, and all my colleagues knew the details of the affair by heart. The point was simply to thrash out an interpretation that would be at once theoretically indisputable, factually exhaustive, and ultimately reasonable.

As far as method went, ours recalled, in a way, that of Rashomon: confronting contradictory visions of the truth. But instead of looking at reality through the prism of each participant's experience, we tried to examine it meticulously in the light of one decision theory after another. Theory, of course, is abstract, it has rough edges and it distorts the facts. Its power of explanation always falls short of what a good journalistic analysis can do. But to abandon it is to fall back upon . . . journalistic analysis: determining who the good guys and the bad guys were, describing what each side had in mind, explaining

[1]*The Essence of Decision: Explaining the Cuban Missile Crisis* (Boston: Little, Brown, 1971).

how the troublemakers' evil plans naturally got the upper hand, unmasking the real villain.

By contrast, our seminar aimed at avoiding an overly facile retrospective explanation as well as the moralizing that almost always goes with it, so as to understand the reasons for things at the moment they were happening. In the affair we were studying, there seemed to be no insurmountable obstacles toward reaching this goal: everybody agreed that the decision made was a good one, the evil schemes had not triumphed, there was no need to search for the guilty party. Our attempt could not be disturbed by the fascinating lure of evil.

The fact, then, was that the hawks had failed to use the crisis to get their revenge for the Bay of Pigs and to wipe out Cuba once and for all. But why did they lose out? Analysis showed that the balance of power by no means favored the doves, who were actually just as much the losers here. The solution could definitely not be found by exploring Kennedy's psychology or intentions, but rather by analyzing how the problem had been framed and how, in responding to it, the protagonists had made use of their different advantages, especially their competence and their imagination.

The hawks lost out because they had failed to understand the whole issue properly, owing to their intrinsic limitations. The president had been deceived by Khrushchev, who had deliberately lied. And the proofs of that lie were going to come out right in the middle of an election campaign, scandalously contradicting the president's reassuring statements. Kennedy, therefore, had no choice but to react, and strongly. So the hawks had a golden opportunity, since they were in the best position for supplying this sort of response. After having scrutinized various peaceful solutions, which seemed totally inadequate, the National Security Council looked into the least dangerous of the military solutions: a "surgical" air attack, which would destroy the Soviet rockets without threatening the urban population or the Castro regime. But the hawks were not an abstract entity; in this case they were, to be precise, the air force, which had a certain number of programs and experts at their disposal. And their blueprints obviously made no provision for anything like a surgical attack: the experts declared that they could not guarantee the success of such an operation. From their point of view the only reasonable response would be to liquidate the Castro regime. There was no time to check out their argument (later, when time allowed, the air force experts were proved wrong). But the air force people, who thought they had won and finally had the president where they wanted him, were forced to change their tune when Kennedy rejected this solution and ordered the military to keep on looking for another one. This allowed the navy to come up with *their* solution, which was tough but much less dangerous: quarantine the Soviet ships.

So the navy, one might think, had shown themselves to be doves, and that that is what altered the balance of power. Not at all: the navy was no less hawkish than the air force. In fact, they exploited the situation by launching some particularly dangerous operations that until then they had been forbidden to carry out, such as pursuing Soviet submarines all through the oceans of the world. This branch of the armed forces, with less speed at its command, was simply unwilling to forgo the chance to score so stunning a victory over the air force.

And while all this was going on, what happened to the actual doves? Well, they lost out, too, not from any lack of intelligence or preparation but because all the diplomatic solutions called for time, which was no longer available because of the CIA's tardiness in verifying the information about the missile installations in Cuba. Aha, the reader might say, now we have the villain, the CIA. But it was not even their fault: if the CIA was behind schedule, that was because they were working under constraints laid down by Congress and the president and because of interservice squabbles. And no one could be in favor of weakening these restraints. After seriously considering the problem, one could not even propose to restructure the intelligence services with the aim of perfecting their efficiency. That would entail an immense risk, since only the war among the various intelligence services makes it possible to oversee each one and, ultimately, to be sure that the information they provide is credible. To rationalize intelligence gathering would be to set up a dictatorship over information. The price of escaping such a dictatorship is a certain slowness of operation, and one must accept paying that price.

What all this adds up to is that there is no absolute rationality, only partial and contingent rationalities, all bound up with circumstances. To understand the choices men make, one must understand both the topography of the problems and the spectrum of possible solutions. This means taking into account not only the chief power blocs and their interests but also their habits and capabilities, and noting as well the rules of the political and administrative game, paying less attention to programs and party platforms than to the concrete imperatives that all protagonists, big or little, have to bow to. Thus the good decision maker—for example, a good president—is not the one who has the best ideas, who brings the best intentions to his job, or who pursues the highest ambitions. Jimmy Carter's motto "Why not the best?" opens up a fast track to disaster. The good decider is the one who has clearly grasped the structure of the problems to be solved and who manages to set up a decision-making system that is sufficiently open, imaginative, and able to find the least bad solution, given the inherent constraints in the situation.

Those years, so full of surprises and discoveries, witnessed the beginnings of an intellectual invasion of the so-called serious world. Everything seemed possible. The sort of seminar I attended was the heart of the recently founded Kennedy School of Government at Harvard whose lofty mission was to train the statesmen of tomorrow (Graham Allison was to become its second dean). People at the Kennedy School thought they had time to spare, but the drama that would sweep so much away had already begun.

Still, I do not wish to disown the work they did in Cambridge and the things they believed in. They were men of goodwill, acting in good faith. They were trying to bring reason—and consequently skepticism—to bear on the illusions of triumphant rationality, without yet realizing the limits of the world they had entered. My colleagues were not lacking in courage, and they knew how to maintain a certain distance from their subject. Some of them went down to "consult" in Washington a bit too often, but they kept a cool head. One day Johnson offered one of them, Thomas Schelling, a special assignment aimed at reorganizing the State Department. Tom is an admirable intellectual. He has a serious, honest, open look. His whole being seems to be reflected in his face, and that almost disembodied face is the very image of rationality. He worked for a few weeks, then convened the seminar. He told us, in essence, that the State Department was beyond reform. The only reasonable move would be to close it down, but that was certainly not one of the choices available to the president. So he intended to refuse the job. In the long, passionate, and rather comical discussion that followed I was surprised to find myself almost the only one willing to argue on behalf of Foggy Bottom. European timidity? Respect for established institutions? In any event, against everyone else in the seminar I defended, in vain, the case for complication, delay, and wasting time.

In those days Henry Kissinger was playing war games with the generals in the Pentagon. With his far too intimate ties to the Republicans, he was not one of us, but his old friend Stanley Hoffmann kept the lines of communication open. Every week Kissinger went to Washington and came back to Cambridge all aglow: with that enormous modesty, the overwhelming simplicity that will earn him a place in history, he told us how he beat the generals at every turn. They had power, but Henry met force with pure intelligence. *Cedant arma togae,* intelligence will always prevail. The arrogance of the Lone Reasoner began to look threatening.

In the Beginning Was the Harvard Business School

The little world of Cambridge, Massachusetts, revolves around one central spot: Harvard Square. With its Metropolitan Transit Authority station and its newspaper stands, the Square has only a symbolic interest. But it is the hub of American intellectual life, a little like Saint-Germain-des-Prés. Right alongside the Square is Harvard Yard, with its tall trees, its administration buildings, the various college departments, lecture halls, classrooms, and one of the largest university libraries in the world. Beyond, but not far off, lie two other, slightly less important focal points: "across the [Charles] River" is the Harvard Business School, and "down the road" (Massachusetts Avenue) is the Massachusetts Institute of Technology, with its bands of engineers and technocrats striding through its neoclassical facades and functional boxes. So engineers, businessmen (and women), and just plain intellectuals all have their own temple within these sacred precincts— a solid triangle that misunderstandings and countless suspicions have never been able to topple.

Anyone who wishes to understand modern rationality American style, in its greatness and its limitations, must go across the river to take a look. Harvard Business School is not a professional school in the European manner, one of those sham institutions where students learn a variety of techniques that turn out to be useless once final exams are over, and where the only items of value graduates get for their trouble are the connections they make and the title of alumnus. On the contrary, HBS is a genuine school, where people know what they are looking for—and find it—a factory of sorts, a marvelous factory turning out (under pitiless quality control) those products of high technology: decision makers, superb machines capable of swallowing an incredible mass of data and variables, and then using them to reach the optimal decision. The process of manufacturing these executives is a form of teaching in which, the content, naturally, counts for a great deal, but so does the method it inculcates, a method that is simple, robust, unchangeable—and, above all, elusive (and yet essential), something akin to true religion.

The content, which might not seem all that inaccessible, deals principally with evaluating results of human activities and the best means of employing the available resources, to achieve those results. This presents a crucial problem, owing to the internal complexity of large modern companies and, above all, to the even greater complexity of the environment in which they evolve. Thus, beyond a certain stage of operations, the market is no longer a sufficiently precise sanction. It indicates to what extent products are competitive but not why. It does not enable management to determine the respective contribution of each factor in production, nor to settle the contradictory claims of the people in charge of various aspects of a business, all of whom offer excellent arguments for getting more investments, that is, a larger share of total resources.

Then there is the basic contradiction affecting the size of companies. Success implies ever increasing expansion and power, which make it possible to rationalize production and purchasing, to lower manufacturing costs, and so crush weaker competitors—the pattern of the ineluctable concentration of capital, familiar to us from Marxian analysis. Nonetheless, the more important a company is, the less it controls its own activity. It tends to get lost in the bureaucratic maze and to become lazy and inefficient. The logical limit to this development is the perfect monopoly, as in the Soviet Union where the general economic chaos ultimately forced the government to use American prices so as to have at least a rough measuring stick of its economy.

How to remain active and efficient without renouncing growth is the foremost problem facing modern organizations. In an effort to solve it they commonly bring the market into their midst, not the concrete market, of course, which is too cumbersome, but an abstract substitute, enabling one to calculate the exact contribution of each unit and each function and to gauge its performance. This has nothing to do with decentralization in the political sense; it is simply an especially severe system of internal auditing. American consultants have made their reputation with this model, and firms like MacKinsey have been importing it to Europe since the mid-sixties.

Still, placing special emphasis on the environment brings two other decisive features to light: comparison of operations and evolution of operations over time. These features can serve as the basis of a system different from the preceding one, a system which is much praised by the new wave of consultants and which is now successful the world over: the strategic model of decision making. Here the objective becomes choosing the best possible "portfolio" of operations. Both doctrines came out of the Harvard Business School. Both have flourished; because both are very simple and very practical, their implementation pays immediate dividends and, furthermore, they take advantage of a particularly efficient method of teaching and communication.

The teaching method followed at the Harvard Business School is known all over the world as the case study approach. Its true birth-place was the Harvard Law School where future lawyers are trained not by analyzing texts but by solving problems. "Across the river" this method has to reckon with the tremendous complexity of choices in business matters as well as by the factors of uncertainty and future projection. It makes it possible to have a clearer view of the issues by using a sort of intellectual simulation, and among the students broad-ens the spectrum of possibilities, at the same time that it subjects each one of the participants to the unsparing judgment of the group. Every student has to work like a madman if he wants to maintain his rank in the group: night after night he studies a hundred pages or so to prepare his cases, to find solutions that he will later have to defend against the carping critique of his comrades and rivals. This group maieutic exercise is fearfully efficient and had placed the Harvard Business School among the most formidable institutions ever erected by human genius, alongside the Jesuit order and the Prussian High Command.

But the school's success does not owe simply to a pedagogy whose rich and concrete content goes hand in hand with a method of proven efficacy. That in itself would mean little if this training did not also develop an esprit de corps and a coherent set of values that one cannot help comparing with a religion. That may seem surprising, since the HBS nurses no ideological ambitions and has no other goal than the quite basic one of educating students to respond to the demands of business. Despite this, I have never met any teachers more firmly convinced of the importance of their mission or students more pro-foundly indoctrinated. What is really at stake here is not so much learning to make money as finding the exact solution. The god being worshiped is not the Golden Calf, as one might suspect, but rationality. Trying to make a big killing, profiting from a privileged situation to get a guaranteed unearned income, filling one's pockets and then making a quick exit from the casino—here such behavior is judged immoral and behind the times. There is no need to go through Har-vard Business School for *that*. Business, needless to say, is still business, and the young MBAs will not fail to learn all the tricks of the trade from the old-timers, many of whom will not have been to graduate school. But the religion of rationality goes far beyond business; in principle, no realm at all is foreign to it.

This religion is what the whole world converted to in the middle sixties. Europe, Japan, and soon all dynamic countries caught the fever. In the United States itself every sphere of activity—administration, education, health, public assistance—seemed on the verge of a profound renewal. Thus the Kennedy School of Government had as its central article of faith that it was possible to discover rational methods for political and administrative decisions. Every aspect of education appeared to be susceptible to a brilliant transformation, not only through better management of financial resources but also through improvement of the process itself: analysis of the way educational programs are carried out reveals that an extravagant amount of time is wasted on providing a mediocre transmission of irrelevant information, whereas the really useful message never gets across. Rationalizing the whole endeavor, so as to concentrate better on the main purpose, could increase the yield tenfold. To those who waxed indignant over so technocratic a perspective, the answer was given that precisely because human capital is by far the most precious kind, it is essential not to squander it.

Reason's Lonely Frontier

Looking backward, Robert McNamara seems to have been the exemplary figure in that powerful trend toward rationality. But his stunning talents as an intellectual machine should not make us overlook the unusual man who possessed them: active, balanced, brave, candid, and whatever his detractors may have said with a more than usually tender conscience, he was in many ways modest and simple. There was some arrogance in his tendency to lose his patience in arguments over figures, where he recognized no equal. His career, though certainly illustrious, was not particularly varied or eventful. In 1939 he was a young professor at the Harvard Business School with a reputation as a genius in statistical control. During the war he served in the air force and, along with other young technocrats, played a pivotal role in building and setting afloat the most gigantic armada of all time—and this despite a federal administration that was as lethargic as the one that was responsible in France for losing the war to the Germans. Besides not finding a McNamara, France unfortunately could not rely on time nor on an ocean to protect itself.

After V-J Day McNamara and seven of his colleagues offered their services to the Ford company, which was in need of a complete overhaul: the immense bureaucracy set up by Henry Ford on a supercentralized feudal model had been losing money for twenty years.

47

Young Henry Ford II, the founder's grandson, seized power in a palace revolution, but that was not enough to dissipate the cloud of confusion enveloping that enormous empire. In order to get out from under and once and for all get a clearer view of the situation, management had to start from scratch, examining each area of operations one by one. Where were they losing money, and why? Who was making the decisions? With what consequences and at what risks? McNamara was not the least bit interested in automobiles as such, and supposedly prided himself on not knowing how a car was made. But the problem was not one of production, which was the exclusive bailiwick of the technicians. McNamara could not have cared less about carburetors or chrome or hubcaps, but he knew how to count and how to create order and efficiency. So he was forgiven for belonging to another world, for living in Ann Arbor like the intellectuals, for taking an interest in all sorts of things—even the future of the automotive industry or the degree of safety provided by a given car model.

He brought with him what management needed the most: an aptitude for getting a grip on costs and benefits. Eventually Henry Ford decided to let him have the presidency of the company, but just after being appointed McNamara was called to Washington to meet the newly elected John F. Kennedy. After a half-hour interview in Detroit in a miracle of American dispatch, he was hired to tame the Pentagon bureaucracy.

Every government, in every country of the world, has to face this insoluble problem: the drain on the national budget by military expenditures always seems too great, though for all that the defense system cannot be considered truly satisfactory. So it is imperative to reduce expenses. But how? Any attempt to cancel a program, even an utterly minor one, provokes an outcry. Across the board budgetary reductions, or putting a ceiling on all outlays, can lead to aimless cuts, which only increase waste. To keep pace with the general escalation and maintain its ability to defend the country the government is forced to invest in new armament systems. The only solution consists in getting a clear, complete readout of how funds are used, or at least in employing the supervision that can relate expenditures to the actual usefulness of each operation within the colossal machine.

As in his Ford years, McNamara had the job of helping to clear up the picture, of introducing order and rationality into a proliferating bureaucracy, to set back on track a machine whose gigantic size had driven it out of control. The idea was not so much to spend less as to spend better, to slash unproductive expenses in favor of more productive ones. The questions were: What's this good for? Couldn't we do it differently? The Rand Corporation had perfected a method for transferring cost/benefit analysis from business to the public sphere, and the first item on McNamara's agenda at Defense was to put young researchers from Rand in key posts.

Long-time federal bureaucrats viewed this effort as heroic but hopeless. Naturally, it was only half successful, but it still led to some tangible, and occasionally spectacular, results. A fresh wind blew through the federal administration. The procedure called for two steps: a systems analysis (of relationships among major objectives, among secondary objectives, and the nature and purpose of detailed operational programs) and a comparative cost/benefit analysis of those minute concrete programs.

On the one hand the problems facing the Defense Department looked insurmountable: a formidable technical and administrative labyrinth and a veritable jungle of petty suzerainties, with each bureau linked to clients represented by senators and congressmen, all representing a military-congressional complex even more stubborn than the military-industrial complex once denounced by Eisenhower. On the other hand, the military people proved to be much more cooperative than expected and did not resist for very long. In fact, these honest, obedient technocrats, far less devious than the average bureaucrat or politician, have an undeserved reputation for extreme conservatism. They managed, certainly, to domesticate the invading forces and tame their method, but what is important is that they adopted it, forcing Congress to follow suit and convert to the religion of rational calculation. Often enough the results fell way short of initial hopes, but something had stirred! McNamara had opened the door to a critical change.

By the time Johnson came to power McNamara had become indispensable. There was no rapport between him (still loyal to the Kennedys) and the new president (who hated them). But Johnson was fascinated by McNamara's intellectual powers and enthusiastic over his method, which Johnson needed to realize his grand design. He decreed that the Planning Programming Budgeting System, as the Rand method was called, would be the fundamental principle of organization for the entire federal administration and called for its overall use by state and local administrations.

Johnson thought that in this way he could maintain his grandiose vision of the Great Society while fighting the war in Vietnam. He hoped that because of McNamara, the administrators would follow his lead. Unfortunately, even with McNamara, the administrators could do nothing of the sort. The war in Vietnam was sinking into quicksand, for reasons that had nothing to do with cost/benefit analysis. Civilian affairs obviously did not raise problems of conscience, but in a sense they suffered even more omnipresent disorder. If nothing else, defense matters are governed by a certain number of constraints, a reality principle, so to speak. War makes all meanings ambiguous and falsifies all calculations, but, apart from the specific conflict, the principal objective remains: to do at least as well and if possible a little better than the enemy, the Soviet Union. The military has a clear notion of where it is headed; it can give the taxpayers—thanks to the methods of budgetary rationalization—the assurance that they will have the best possible defense consistent with their fiscal mandate.

Civilian affairs are much less clear because the goals being pursued inevitably remain obscure: no one has ever been able to explain what a society, generally speaking, is for. Besides, to get a legislative measure passed in a democratic system, it is essential to preserve a degree of ambiguity both as to objective and to wording. Then, too, the various measures passed at sundry times, or even simultaneously, more often than not contradict one another. Taking each one of them literally leads to chaos. To prevent that from happening, one must know how much weight to assign the different values inspiring the concrete measures: social peace, justice (subject to many interpretations), the well-being of the most deprived, full employment, economic development, and so on. People want it all and all at the same time, knowing it to be all bound up together but in no way understanding how. Technocratic clarity only raises a host of problems, commonly insoluble ones, without improving our knowledge of the human reality that all the statistical studies are supposed to be describing.

There were a few spectacularly wrongheaded moves, such as the order to apply the PPBS to all State Department operations, hence to all diplomatic stations abroad. Within a few months diplomats were laboriously trying to keep records on the ways they used their time, distributing it under various bureaucratic headings, or evaluating their friendly connections in the country in which they were serving in the light of cost/benefit analysis. And even in the much more numerous cases where such exercises made sense, the upshot was a glaring failure in the long run, for reasons that we shall see.

In passing, however, let me stress that this experiment was far from being totally useless, and that it gave rise to a vast quantity of new ideas and original solutions, some of whose implications have yet to be developed. Sometimes, too, decisions worked out in this way proved to be excellent for reasons altogether different from the ones that had prompted them. For example, lowering the speed limit achieved only meager savings in energy but dramatically reduced the highway death toll. After the fact, to look at it from another angle, the benefits realized can be quantified, at the risk of causing some offense: who, except a soulless technocrat, would want to estimate the value of a human life? Still, if statistical studies enable us to prove that a given rational measure can save three thousand people from dying each year, then long live statistical studies.

Similarly, expenditures for health and even for research have provided some splendid food for thought, not only in America but subsequently in all of Western Europe and Japan. Why then did these methods, which led to a better understanding of the facts in more than one domain, fail to result in applications that were really well suited to their environment? There are two main reasons for the failure. The first is that everybody cheats: through a system of public relations and unnatural alliances when there are hopes of getting a given measure passed; and through individual arrangements or collective pull at the point of implementation. No sacred principle, no fear of the police ever stops people from cheating in this fashion.

The second reason is that everywhere one finds coming into play complex human systems, which exist prior to administrative action and, although they may be thrown into disarray by it, quickly reconstruct themselves afterward under another guise. These systems follow guidelines different from those of the cost/benefit analysis, and the attempt to rationalize them, far from helping to understand the way they work, tends to destroy their characteristic regulatory mechanisms. From this standpoint, the temptation to arrogance on the part of would-be custodians of the truth becomes particularly dangerous. The modesty often affected by technocrats changes nothing here, because at issue is a more profound form of arrogance. Thus, in the Johnson years the policies of all those brilliant apostles of rationality gradually lost sight of the most elementary common sense.

Nationalism and Liberalism

Whereas under Kennedy the federal administration may have seemed hard to govern, twenty years later it appears to be the ne plus ultra of inefficiency and confusion, to a point bordering on absurdity pure and simple. That is why France, which is very familiar with the problem, has still to see an explosion of bitterness, indignation, and rage among its citizens like the one that has shaken the United States.[2]

[2]This explosion is gradually mounting now after two years of Socialist government.

51

Many Americans think that Washington is now beyond reform. More than a handful would also like to see the whole federal government abolished.

This reaction is playing an increasingly large role in political life. One of Jimmy Carter's main themes during his 1976 election campaign was the reform of the federal bureaucracy. Many of the realities he entertained as a pious technocrat have since been buried in the Circumlocution Office, but, for all that, "deregulation" has lately become a magic word in Washington. Systematic efforts were being made to dismantle the major federal regulatory commissions, which, especially in the areas of transportation, communications, and environment, wrapped all activities in an iron web of countless regulations. And in America, unlike France, these rules are enforced to the letter by squads of lawyers totally lacking in the French virtue of skepticism.

The Republicans are naturally the ones who roar the loudest in their condemnation of Washington and who expect to benefit the most from this popular mood. Apart from a long and highly simplistic reactionary tradition that fuels their rhetoric, in recent years the GOP has gotten fresh support of a quite different intellectual quality: the economists of the Milton Friedman school, the "libertarians" of all species who preach direct control of all activities by citizens themselves, and the neoconservatives, who blast the failure of a liberalism they see as increasingly mired in bureaucracy.

In the face of this seeming convergence between the two major parties, Teddy Kennedy was for some time the only major political figure to fight openly and vigorously for the traditionally liberal Democratic position. But the trend does not go in his direction and even some of his most faithful friends alarmed by the success of John Anderson among the young and the middle class liberals warned of the danger. The 1984 campaign seems to accentuate the same pattern with Walter Mondale arguing the liberal creed but in a more lukewarm and defensive way and Gary Hart trying to capitalize on the new trend. The future no longer seems to belong to social programs, to technocratic intervention in the economy to safeguard jobs, to looking after the interests of minorities, to all these centrally administered measures, which were designed for the welfare of all society and which distinguished the great tradition of American liberalism. No one dares anymore to try to justify a federal bureaucracy which everyone's rhetoric calls intrusive and absurd. The Democrats are on the defensive because they represent the innumerable groups and minorities that make up the clientele of that gigantic enterprise—the federal government. How did it come to this? How did the cult of clarity and rationality that reigned supreme in the sixties give way to this widespread disenchantment and, concretely, to the breakdown of government activity?

It is impossible to answer those questions without reflecting on history—the history the course of which America believed had come to a halt and which had taken its revenge. The cult of rationality fed on the illusion that one could obtain a complete knowledge of the facts and thereby determine the best solution—which people would end up accepting because it was the best, once the complications, difficulties, and the manipulative habits that still hang heavy on human relations had all been surmounted. Then democracy and rationality would converge in a world become transparent. Then democracy would oversee the making of choices, whose total implementation rationality would empower.

It was the return, in a sense, of a very old dream. McNamara had rediscovered the utopian tradition. Frederick W. Taylor and Henry Ford before him had thought they could substitute the administration of things for the government of men. The work of my colleagues at Harvard obviously ran counter to this illusion, but they were borne along by so powerful a wave of faith that their skepticism, which I shared, could do nothing to weaken the tremendous optimism with which, despite everything, they too were imbued.

Americans had believed for too long in the virtue of free arrangements among the parties concerned: let the various interests and factions negotiate among themselves, and little by little, by trial and error, they will find the best solution. Through a device similar to Adam Smith's "invisible hand," every individual, in seeking his own interest, involuntarily promotes the common good. The advent of rational calculation offered a fresh challenge to this logic, whose weak points were only too evident. When the short term is systematically preferred over the long term, it certainly does make for the best possible arrangement here and now, but today's success is often tomorrow's disaster. And there is no proof that the system will ever learn by experience.

Everything would be for the best if it could be continually reformed, but the predominance of the technocrats is of next to no help, because they are incapable of understanding the system with any depth, and they only complicate it under the pretext of clarifying it, forcing once open arrangements to become clandestine and thus much harder to scrutinize. In this way we are left with the worst combination imaginable: a facade of technocratic moralism over a system of clandestine structures which defies surveillance, refuses to let any information leak out, and flounders in the ruts it started out in. The Vietnam War, in a way, fits this model to a "T." In the end, as a result of wanting to decide all matters under conditions of perfect clarity, one ultimately leaves them to the bureaucrats, with their hunger and thirst for abstract justice, to regulate in a complicated and costly fashion, problems for which the people concerned would have spontaneously found more efficient answers.

Still, the current reaction to the rationalist model is no less absurd. Can anyone seriously believe that the principles espoused by Milton Friedman will straighten out the American system of education, now declining, or even make the American economy competitive again? One can play tricks with the market as well as with the law or with bureaucratic procedures. It is no way for society to become a transparent system, always making optimal adjustments on the basis of ideally accurate information. Technocracy, to be sure, lost no time in reaching the threshold past which it goes insane, but the hubris of the politicians is no less dangerous.

As for the businessmen, they would eventually cut their own throats, if left to themselves. Turning 180 degrees away from something is not the same as actually leaving it behind.

CHAPTER FOUR

WILL HAPPY DAYS
BE HERE AGAIN?

**The World of
Shangri-La**

THE SEASONED TRAVELER landing in the United States three years after Ronald Reagan's inauguration as president may be forgiven a certain skepticism about America's constantly changing moods, for once again he is taken by surprise. Strange impressions assail him. Much is just as it was when Jimmy Carter left office, and yet it is as if the clock had been turned back twenty-five years. "Happy days are here again." It is difficult to put one's finger on the change, but there is something in the air, something in the way people talk to one another. Not that Americans have become enthusiastic again. They remain cautious. They seem to fear becoming hyperactive again. But there is courtesy and some mild optimism in their caution. They talk business, business as usual. And money. Money comes up everywhere. Not the way to make more money but the way to make the best of it.

It is as if a gigantic sobering-up had taken place, and we were awakening on the morning after. The big storm has passed, and under a fresh blue sky we move slowly to readjust.

It is slightly ironic to discover that the man who presides over the return to this populist, happy days mood is a Republican president and a man whom many have regarded as a right-wing extremist. But the young Ronald Reagan was a Rooseveltian Midwesterner, and he has kept the easy, infectious smile and the simple American values of past happy days.

The America of the eighties wants to forget history. It pretends that nothing dramatic has ever happened. Everybody will find his old place again, and the nation is going to remain forever the same.

Was John F. Kennedy really murdered on November 22, 1963? America almost begins to doubt it. After all, President Reagan was shot on March 30, 1981, again by a bizarre young crackpot. A real remake, just like in the movies! But a remake with a happy ending. This time, everything is as it should be. The star comes up after the shot and shows his cool head and sense of humor by cracking two good jokes. The jokes make the headlines. The Dallas tragedy is exorcised.

Presidents should not matter so much especially during a period allegedly devoted to a return to the business-as-usual ideal. But they do. Then, more than ever, they express the country's longings. With the rugged, smiling face of an old Hollywood cowboy, Ronald Reagan will take his place in the American legend, especially since he is embodying a version of the American eternity, of the unending American happy days. Television screens showed the painful process of aging on the faces of Johnson, Nixon, and Carter. These were tormented presidents, haunted by fate, divided against themselves, ambivalent and uncertain. Reagan appears unalterable, protected forever against adversity. He is as young, as calm, as sure of himself as when he was inaugurated. He shows no doubts and no ambivalence. At the ranch, at the White House, at a party, or before the TV screen to address the American people, he is always his simple and natural self. His acting is superb. He looks quintessentially human, especially when his loving wife gives him the admiring look that befits a real hero. There is no better image of the happy days all Americans want for themselves and for their country.

His enemies of course insist that such happy days are first of all the happy days of the millionaires, which is partly true. But they forget that most Americans still feel in the deepest part of their unconscious selves that one day they may be millionaires too. And even those who vote against Reagan are still somewhat touched by his charm. They may explain it away by emphasizing the professional qualities of the "Great Communicator." But they certainly are not immune to it.

Once past this basic impression of the return of the happy days, however, one encounters another less striking but more pervasive impression of irreality beneath the surface of things. This is especially true if one focuses on the political world.

Reagan and his team embody the happy days mood. This much is clear. And they are successful at it, but only in a sort of Hollywood way. To do this may be to perform a good and helpful service, but it is to soothe America rather than to express its real reactions. Sometimes the visitor fears that this is government by dreams. When deficits, high interest rates, and economic recovery are associated as by magic, the whole political debate seems "way up in the air," divorced from reality.

There is, in short, a kind of Shangri-la atmosphere over America. It may be at its heaviest in Washington, but it is floating all over the continent, in the communications systems, in the movies, on TV, and even in the new wonders of the computer world. Like James Hilton's mythical Himalayan city that caught the public imagination just before World War II, Reagan's America has managed to make time stand still. In Shangri-la people were to be eternally young because they were protected from history and tragedy; that is, from evil. Human relations were forever happy. Nothing ever happened.

One feels this sort of Hollywood make-believe consensus in Reagan's America. The nation that forgot the past is fighting to forget the future. A manly and cheerful president will forever ride horses and enforce the law while the country will tend its business the way it always has, and the world will be forced back to peace because America is as strong and determined as its president is.

The Craving for Normalcy

Ronald Reagan has his own style, a very successful one indeed. But he is not imposing anything on the American people against their will. Rather he succeeds ultimately because he has perceived the people's demands and answered them as only a good professional can.

The dream of happy days exists everywhere. Since Adam fell, man's basic demand has been to return to Eden. Man does not like history. He would like it to stop so that he might live for himself in the forever-after time of happiness. Marxists proclaimed their scientific way to achieve the end of history, but they were just coming back to the same ageless fairy tale. Just like happy people, happy nations have no history.

But Americans have had a very special relationship to that age-old illusion. The longing for the happiness of the steady state could be stronger for them because in a certain sense it was justified. The new settlers in America had fled Old World quarrels, religious wars, oppressive states, and the concomitant sense of history as well. The new nation they intended to found was to be a nation of innocence, and the new society they built was at least a step in that direction. Its principles worked, and its general consensus on good and evil helped reject fate and history. Opposition and conflicts there were aplenty, to be sure, but neither bitter enough nor rooted deeply enough in tribal tradition to make real history. Americans proudly felt they had achieved the steady state. Other less advanced nations had to suffer power struggles, drama, civil wars, coups of all sorts that fitted their archaic, conflict-ridden societies. Americans knew how to behave in a more civilized manner. They had moved from bloody history to aseptic evolution.

This rosy picture was of course largely false. The American Civil War was as bloody as any European war, and the Gettysburg address still echoes in school children's minds. Yet a generally happy ahistorical attitude still pervades the American mind, public as well as the private. Individual logic, popular feeling, and government reasoning are all affected. The dramas of a finite world that must live with the impending threat of death are as by instinct rejected from this forever happy, ongoing world of the present; likewise power relations with their implications of blackmail cannot be recognized as natural and unavoidable. Evil has no real existence. It is simply the result of misunderstanding, backwardness, and cultural lag.

Such a feeling was reawakened to the point of exacerbation, it seems to me, with the extraordinarily long years of sound and fury the country had to endure from Kennedy's assassination through the Vietnam War and Watergate to the seizure of the hostages in Tehran. In these problems of collective psychology, too little attention has been paid to the effect of the passing of time. Eleven years elapsed from the Dallas murder to the end of Watergate, and seventeen till the release of the hostages. These are very long periods indeed, much longer than either the American or the English revolution. Longer even than the French revolution proper,[1] in any case very much longer than the American Civil War and the two World Wars. These comparisons may look shocking since the period does not look nearly as

---

[1] From Bastille Day to the consolidation of Bonaparte, fifteen years elapsed; twenty-five elapsed from Bastille to the restoration of the Bourbon king.

eventful as a "real revolution" and is of course much less bloody than these great wars. However, if one cares for the real impact, many close observers already maintain that the traumas have been as deep and in a certain sense deeper. Antagonistic emotions were aroused to the point of genuine collective passions. Minds were perturbed deeply, cherished beliefs shattered. The end results finally were not as important in that case as the processes and what it meant for Americans.

In any event, such periods of intensity of feelings cannot last very long. They become gradually unbearable. Escalation may be a way out at the beginning. Each new cohort of young zealots outsmarts its elders by becoming more daring and more radical; but once the ceiling has been hit, it is no longer possible to win in such a game. People will now begin to compete in skepticism instead of competing in radicalism and a basic fashion change will take place.

Other countries have known the backlash movements of these great fashion shifts. Back-to-normalcy movements have accompanied postwar and postrevolutionary periods. America itself knew this after the Civil War and in the twenties and in the fifties. But this time it was to be much stronger, as if an irresistible craving verging on the pathological would sweep everything away. The main reason for it has been time, the long delays with two earlier abortive attempts to reverse the trend, but also something new: the merging of a back-to-normalcy craving with a much more deeply idealized yearning to return to a happy state which never existed and is of course unattainable.

Gerald Ford first, then Jimmy Carter, could have led the country to a more moderate back-to-normalcy movement, and they tried hard. It is worthwhile to enquire why they failed. Gerald Ford came too early or at least was too candid in his attempt at forgiving the sins of the past. People wanted to forget, not to forgive. Jimmy Carter could perhaps have made it but for his bad luck and for a sort of Hamletian quality in him, an indecisiveness that cried out for failure. And something else is worth remembering: if Ford was ready to settle all accounts too easily, Carter was too utterly uncompromising. His aim of purity, his lofty ideals, his posture as "Mister Clean" as exemplified in the naive title of his public relations book *Why Not the Best?* retained the same megalomaniac trait that had ruined his predecessors' best intentions.

In view of those failures, Ronald Reagan's success is all the more impressive. There was to begin with a basic dilemma to solve. Should one follow a "normal" back-to-normalcy course; that is, adjust to the world as it is? This is what was offered in the cautious-conservative, uninspiring Ford days. Or should one try to bring back The-World-As-It-Should-Be; that is, the Pax Americana of the fifties?

Reagan did not by any means solve the dilemma, but he has led the way out of it. This is the real meaning of his Hollywood style. One should not be too harshly critical. Soothing may be temporarily the best course. After a nervous breakdown, a lot of sleep and rest is necessary. Illusions and dreams may help provide that needed sleep and rest. After all, General de Gaulle led his country out of the traumatic experience of the bitter Algerian war by making it reinvest in its past glories and dreams of excellence. Meanwhile he put the French house in order, put the economy back on its feet, and reasserted the weight of collective responsibilities and the respect due to those who have to bear them.

Ronald Reagan may not have been as successful in circumstances that are in many ways more difficult. But at least two of his achievements stand out as equally strong: the eradication of inflation and the assertion of presidential power against special interests. Inflation cuts at everybody's day-to-day practices. It destroys confidence and trust in human transactions. Groups of all kinds pressure the state, exacting anything they can of the public and in the process destroy the economic game. Reagan's success against inflation and special interests was made possible by his soothing style and in turn gave legitimacy to that style.

I would not like to overemphasize the point, but it seems to me there is a much larger skill in Ronald Reagan's behavior than just the nice Hollywood PR job he is credited with. For that very reason, there is also more danger when problems are not solved, not even advanced. Drifting along in happy-days dreams may be indispensable for some few years, but it will become a source of embarrassment extremely quickly. Moreover, for all that it may lead the country out of its crisis of morale, it may lead it in a gradually more unrealistic direction.

A Numbness in the Air

These contradictions and the problems looming ahead may not be visible yet. But as soon as one scratches the surface of public conventions, one discovers a strange passivity, a lack of commitment, a cautiousness that is in striking contrast with the happy-days mood.

Twenty, thirty years ago, happy days were quite different. Then, people were genuinely optimistic, open, and curious. They believed in the future, their private future as well as the public future. They were expansionists. They built families and businesses as if they were settling new territories. They were proud of their achievements and cared for the public good. The happy days of the eighties are protectionist, even defeatist. People care about their own private world, which they do not associate with the public good. They care about holding their own, if necessary, by defending their interests *against* the public good. There may well be a revival of the entrepreneurial spirit, but for the moment it is limited to certain groups and categories of persons. It is a minority affair that is important economically but not yet significant socially.

Make-believe politics is soothing, but it is not inspiring. It may bring enough votes, but it will not restore basic values. Liberals were frightened by the new wave of conservatism. They visualized cohorts of Moral Majority barbarians taking hold of Washington and systematically destroying all the results painfully achieved in decades of efforts to civilize a rough-and-tumble capitalist society. About this, they were just plain wrong. The will to change the American economy and society in a conservative direction may be present, but there is no strong movement behind it. Why? Because there is no strong mass movement of *any* sort possible for the moment. Because Americans do not care enough, liberalism has lost its momentum. But the New Right has lost its own small momentum as well. No "Conservative Revolution" is possible because Americans are just uninterested in politics of any kind. Ronald Reagan has been extremely careful and skillful to provide first of all calm, only secondarily change, and even then only such change as provides more calm.

The real test is the mood of the young people who—as always and everywhere—exemplify, exaggerate, and anticipate the trends of society.

"They don't have that gleam in their eyes anymore." A black leader speaks to me. He is a distinguished, urbane gentleman of about forty-five. He has a Ph.D. in urban planning. He has been president of a big city school board. He embodies the best results of the strong emancipation movement that has swept over and revolutionized American society. He is not one of those flamboyant political characters of the past but a thoughtful, considerate, and responsible leader. There is some sadness in his voice; blacks have achieved a great deal and should be proud of their accomplishment, but there is no drive, no inspiration among young people anymore. Not that they lack a cause or things to do, but one does not see that gleam in the eye which makes the difference.

He talked about black youngsters but recognized immediately

that there is no difference on this basic point with white youth. Everywhere it is the same story. What I had felt so brutally with my Harvard students in 1980 was no exception. Sure, Harvard students may be more articulate and therefore sound more cynical. But they only express the general feeling of helplessness.

Liberal educators and liberals generally have a very hard time adjusting to this major trend-reversal because it seems to contradict their traditional logic and defeats all their most cherished hopes. Permissive education as it was promoted has brought not enlightenment and concern but apathy and conservatism.

Compared with their European and Japanese counterparts, American youngsters learn to take care of themselves much earlier. But they also learn to care only for their personal affairs, however ignorantly they may conceive them. This may mean for many of them a refusal to learn. As Dan Morgan pointed out in a thoughtful series in the *Washington Post,* they will earn good pocket money at the nearest supermarket or hamburger joint rather than do school homework or read about the world or fight for a cause. According to his survey, two-thirds of youths between fourteen and eighteen earn at least $100 a week. Since they are living at home, they are much better off than young adults who want to raise a family.[2] How can one expect them to show concern for the rest of the world and for the public good in any but the most emotionally immature way?

During the long years of student unrest and cultural upheaval, young Americans fought together for liberal causes and against oppression everywhere as well as for their own personal freedom from constraints of all sorts. Their successors today enjoy the results of those struggles, but there is no cause, no movement, no real community for them. Everybody is left free to do his or her own thing without caring about others. This ethical priority of individual "affirmative action" has reached its highest intensity in California. Even consumer surveys show that California youth is more advanced in this respect. James Fallows, the noted journalist and former speech writer for Jimmy Carter, who left the California paradise in search of a harder but richer life, is quite blunt about it: "We young Californians were living in a sort of mist." The myth of Silicon Valley with its young entrepreneurs gives a false picture of Californian behavior. True enough, more people there than anywhere else dream about the jackpot that could come to them. Aside from a tiny minority of creative

[2] Dan Morgan, "Coming of Age in the 80s," *Washington Post,* 27 December 1981, 2 January 1982.

young mavericks, however, this dream is basically a dream of facility, of success without any effort.

The new conservatism of American youth is not a political phenomenon but a cultural one. They reject bureaucracies, big political machines, and trade unions, but they also reject communities. They have nothing against getting rich quick. On the contrary! But their rejections of Big Brother bureaucracy do not redound to the benefit of the entrepreneurial spirit. No, traditional entrepreneurial, basically American values—the respect for effort, the will to succeed by personal achievement, the passion to go beyond one's limits—have, at least temporarily, declined. There is no fighting spirit, no drive to conquer and develop the world. Liberals can and may rejoice in the disappearance of the aggressive imperialist spirit. But with it has also gone the unselfish passion for helping others and the sense of public good and human decency.

Paradoxically, if one looks for the old qualities that were supposedly so typically American, it is among first-generation immigrants that one can find them. Asians are providing an exceptionally large proportion of dedicated students eager to move up in schools and universities. All immigrants, even Latinos, lead in small business entrepreneurship. Horatio Alger is no longer an Anglo-Saxon fairy tale. This part of the American dream is now above all the preserve of Southeast Asian and Latin American refugees.

Whatever the amount of protection any group or society can muster, however, it cannot last forever, for protection is self-defeating in the long run. Prolonged adolescence, too well protected by society, produces adults who have a hard time facing the real world. True, their painful experience will eventually reach back and affect the coming generations. Trends can be and will be reversed. For the moment, however, they still continue.

Toward a Reveille of the Public Spirit

Every country is a land of contrasts, America more so than any other according to the traditional reporting of foreigners, probably because the uninhibited passions of its citizens make these contrasts more visible here than in less unabashed societies. And, sure enough, as soon as the visitor becomes conscious of this general overwhelming trend toward apathy, selfishness, and defeatism, he begins to note here and there little signs of dedication and public-spirited ideas and actions. These are indeed only little signs, but they attract attention. The media have an encouraging attitude toward them. And they seem already to have a vague impact on people, as if to shame them if not yet provoking them to emulation. It is as if a new fashion were slowly in the making and just preparing to take shape, or as if by some natural cycle, after a few fallow years, the earth were ready for a rich new crop.

This movement is not a grass-roots movement as yet. This is an intellectual, elitist first wave. But so, necessarily, are all vanguard movements if you do not equate elitism with social status. A basic change in intellectual fashion seems to have taken place in three or four years which has nothing to do with the political trend although it may have been helped by the return to calmer times. The heavy intellectual conformism of the early seventies is finally giving way. One has only to look at bookstores, especially university ones, to discover the amazing turn of the tide. Gone are the piles of Marxist or pseudo-Marxist social studies books which for so long occupied the shelves. Fading too are the narcissistic psychology books about how to know one's own true self and how to enjoy one thing or another.

The intellectual mood is leading elsewhere, in other more realistic directions: no longer inward, no longer deterministic, much less complaining or denouncing. Here we face no defeatist fashion. On the contrary, this is an investigative one. Conventional ideas about institutions and principles are beginning to be questioned again but in much more practical terms. The problems of education, for example, are not discussed in grandiose moralistic terms. Writers begin to wonder instead about what does or does not work, and how it could work better. Theories about business too are no longer questioned in abstract ways but rather in view of their practical results. In politics and welfare the trend is away from the principles down to consequences. The 1983 best-seller *In Search of Excellence* is a good case in point.[3] It may not be such a good book and in other times might have sold only what the publisher expected, that is, a few thousand copies. But it presented cases of success against the rules, real cases with shrewd human beings who were not the conventional competitive type of manager but people dedicated to something bigger than themselves. In one year it caught the public spirit to the point of selling more than one million copies.

The emerging new spirit is not self-doubt in the anxious and driven way of the Carter malaise speech nor is it the self-deprecating spirit of the America-baiting radicals. This is serious, reasonable ques-

[3]Thomas Peters and Robert Waterman, *In Search of Excellence* (New York: Harper & Row, 1982).

tioning that may go deeper if it can persist because it is putting into question self-evident truths. A more secure, more relaxed America may soon be ready for just this questioning.

The education case may be the most dramatic one. No field has been more widely written about and discussed during the last three decades. But what was at stake was the aims of education, its techniques and processes, not its limits, its capacities, and its practical results. What America had wanted was a new more permissive education and, first of all, equality of access. It has now gotten all of that, more or less, but it has discovered that education, meanwhile, has partly disintegrated. Education does not educate anymore. American schools have become inferior to schools in other advanced countries. What is the meaning of equality if it is equality in mediocrity? Minorities discover they have been cheated. What they have achieved with so much pain appears to be hollow because though good education may equalize chances at least partly poor education certainly will not.

The report of the National Commission on Excellence in education will become a landmark in this respect. Its scathing indictment of the American educational system has been a shock. Its true words have been and will be repeatedly quoted.

> We report to the American people that while we can take justifiable pride in what our schools and colleges have historically accomplished and contributed to the United States and well-being of its people, the foundations of our society are presently being eroded by a rising tide of mediocrity that threatens our very future as a nation and a people. . . .

Public reaction is still mixed, but a new debate has clearly emerged. The problem is no longer how to fight injustice, escape guilt feelings, and redeem the world, but how to restore, maintain, and better an institution with its necessary limitations and constraints, without which nothing can ever be achieved.

Articles and books now change focus, and some educators begin to act. Among them, black educators are often in the forefront. Parents who had forgotten the old PTA traditions begin to mobilize again.

As for the American legal system, it has not been the focus of so much attention until recently, although there has been a very general sort of uneasiness about the abuse by lawyers and the complexity of the system. As late as 1979 when Alexander Solzhenitsyn, in a famous Harvard speech, criticized the Western (read *American*) legalistic way of conducting human affairs, he was received extremely coldly.

Four years later the climate has so changed that Derek Bok, president of Harvard University and former dean of the Harvard Law School, as eminent a member of the American legal establishment as can be found, delivers a public report that may be less dramatic in its oratory but certainly is as strong an indictment as the one of the inspired Russian fighter.

Says Bok:

> The blunt inexcusable fact is that this nation which prides itself on efficiency and justice has developed a legal system that is the most expensive in the world yet cannot manage to protect the rights of most of the citizens. . . .
>
> In Japan, a country half our size, 30 per cent more engineers graduate each year than in all the United States. But Japan boasts a total of less than 15,000 lawyers while American universities graduate 35,000 every year. It would be hard to claim that these differences have no practical consequences. As the Japanese put it: engineers make the pie grow larger, lawyers only decide how to carve it up. . . .
>
> This [American legal] environment produces a special kind of justice. It leads officials to exaggerate the law's capacity to produce social change while underestimating the cost of establishing rules that can be enforced effectively throughout the society. Since laws seem deceptively potent and cheap, they multiply quickly. Though most of them may be plausible in isolation, they are often confusing and burdensome in the aggregate at least to those who have to take them seriously.

Here again we have come a very long way from the enthusiasm of the bright young lawyers of the sixties and seventies to fight for justice and equality. The aims were good but the means to be used, the legal system, was defeating them. Now, it is not so much society that is at fault, not even the rich and powerful as a class, among whom one should put the lawyers. Rather it is the institutions that must be reoriented if one does not want further drifting away.

Old taboos are broken also in the business world. One might even suspect that the Japanese challenge in this traditional preserve of American supremacy has been the real trigger to this new soul-searching mood.

The first successful book questioning the American ways has been Ezra Vogel's *Japan as Number One*.[4] His serious and sympathetic account of Japan's reasons for success was clearly pointing to American failures: Japan's respect for knowledge and education, Japan's ex-

---

[4]Ezra Vogel, *Japan as Number One* (Cambridge: Harvard University Press, 1979).

traordinarily well-organized information system, Japan's constant preoccupation with the long term.

The debate has been raging for a few years now but it has been confused because of the importance of related issues: the relevance and complexity of macroeconomic policies; the preoccupation with possible state intervention in industry and its likely consequences; and last but not least, the difficulty of any fair diagnosis of the real situation of American industries.

Pessimistic critics have plenty of arguments: the catastrophic balance of trade deficits, the disastrous decline of the steel industry and other traditional mass production activities, the danger threatening the automobile industry, the deindustrialization of the Northeast and the Midwest, the long decline in productivity.

Optimists counter the argument by pointing out the extraordinary boom of the computer industry and the promises of biogenetics and a score of other high-tech activities. America, so they say, is still in the forefront in all the high-tech industries that are going to count in the future. And this is much more relevant than the decline of the old smokestack factories. Indeed, the second fact is even the condition of the first. Shifting to the policy arguments, many of them show that much of the present plight of a number of very good and high-performing branches is attributable to poor macroeconomic policies that have weakened their capacities to compete. Even extremely well-managed and technologically advanced firms lose market shares consistently through no fault on their part.

The case against an industrial policy may be very strong but it does not mean that the indictment of present theories and practices of American business is wrong. Gradually some new, less conventional views may emerge that will force a general reappraisal of hitherto unchallenged American assumptions.

1. The distinctive American model of unrestrained competition will very often orient the system toward the short term. The Japanese have been able to build the most efficient automobile industry in the world in twenty years because of their capacity to introduce long-term considerations in all their decisions. Meanwhile the American automobile industry has stagnated because all its decisions were short-term oriented. J. K. Galbraith's worries about the capacity of giant corporations to condition demand were plainly ill conceived.[5] Even the strategic rationality of Boston consulting groups seems to lead to abstract portfolio decisions.

[5] J. K. Galbraith, *The New Industrial State* (Boston: Houghton Mifflin, 3d ed., 1979).

2. The dominance of financial and legal considerations in the manufacturing of large corporations tends to stifle the creativity of business. Robert Reich's indictment of paper entrepreneurialism has hit hard. The extravagant case of Martin Marietta versus Bendix happened just at the right time to help the demonstration.[6]

3. At a deeper level many authors now emphasize American business's lack of real concern for the human and institutional aspects of economic life. The renewal of American industry requires that one face the problem of human cooperation. Past enthusiasm for human-relations methods failed because they were drifting always toward PR techniques. Human cooperation is possible only if one understands problems of power, freedom, and leadership. The success of Michael Maccoby's books *The Gamesman* and *The Leader*[7] shows that this concern is now mounting.

Preoccupation with the conditions of innovation is another issue. Pioneers are in demand again. And one begins to understand that there must be pioneering in social issues as well as in technical issues. Change in union-management relationships is a slow and difficult process. But for the first time since the sixties some real progress has taken place under the dire pressure of circumstances.

The Burden of Vietnam and Watergate

A new freedom of the mind is beginning to set in in the sensitive section of American culture where ideas and fashions arise. It is as if something finally has been liberated in the American mind with the return to normalcy. One can only hope now that it will gradually dissipate the delusions of Shangri-la and that a more sensible, realistic, and public-spirited country will finally emerge.

But one basic problem remains which the American mind still has to face and still wants to evade. The lessons are still to be drawn from those fateful years of sound and fury which continue to condition America's posture in the world and the operations of its political and decision-making system.

Americans have of course endlessly debated about who was right and who was wrong. There have been so many reports and accusa-

[6]Ira Mazuzan and Robert Reich, *Minding America's Business* (New York: Harcourt Brace Jovanovich, 1982; Robert Reich, *The Next American Frontier* (New York: Harcourt Brace Jovanovich, 1983).

[7]Michael Maccoby, *The Leader* (New York: Simon and Schuster, 1981); *The Gamesman* (New York: Simon and Schuster, 1976).

tions, so much moral indignation and bitter counterindignation that everybody is tired. Yet there remains the basic problem, at least if one grants some human decency to the fellow whom one would like to use as a scapegoat. The problem: How come the best intentions always led to failure and even disaster? How come American leaders and the American people in general chose the wrong course again and again?

Everything of course begins and ends with the Vietnam War. That was the first real challenge where the nation was tried and found wanting.

Most liberals still continue to address the issue in terms of good and evil: The hawks were the bad guys; the doves were the good guys. The only problem the United States had back then was to drive the hawks from the political scene where they were a disgraceful presence. The only problem now is the same. This simplistic and dangerous notion strikes me as dodging the real issue: How could a country at the zenith of its power, claiming to have the best methods and the best brains available, plunge into so absurd an adventure? Viewed from Europe, with the magnifying glasses of distance and comparative history, the Vietnam War appears to be the result of a curious lapse of foresight and intelligence.

1. It looks in retrospect like the worst strategic error made by the West since Yalta.

2. It looks totally irrational, lacking so much as the excuse of important material interests or a colonial tradition.

With the advantage of hindsight, of course, we can now discern the staggering consequences of this strategic error. In 1962 the United States was the richest and best-armed country in the world. It was still widely respected even in the Third World as the homeland of freedom. In the course of the Cuban missile crisis it had just humiliated the Soviet Union by triumphing through sheer intelligence without using force. Fifteen years later it was retreating on all continents. It had difficulty answering the tremendous Soviet arms buildup in a reasonable, sensible way. Its moral credit in the world had declined sharply. It was divided against itself and in moral disarray at home.

Not all these failures can be ascribed to the Vietnam War; but by its dogged commitment to a secondary theater of operations where it had nothing to gain, the United States gravely compromised its chances for success in a much more vital region, the Middle East, and one may even say weakened its position in its own backyard in Latin America. Beyond that, the enormous sums spent on the Vietnam War threw the international monetary system completely out of kilter while substantially weakening the American economy. Finally and above all, the war sparked an unprecedented moral crisis among the youth of America and then throughout the whole country.

Was it reasonable to risk such catastrophic consequences just to keep within America's sphere of influence a country that while certainly interesting and attractive appeared to feel no special interest for the Western way of life? Here we can attest the enormity of the lapse in intelligence. Despite its tremendous resources for research and planning, the land of triumphant rationality could not even achieve a simple cost/benefit analysis.

When I wonder about this paradox, American friends tend to remind me of our French blunders in Indochina. But we French at least had the excuse of having material and moral interests in this "colony." We were as guilty as colonialists can be, but this was at least to some extent rational. We were attached to our possessions, to what we thought we had achieved over there. It was understandably difficult to forget it and to adjust to the realities of a postcolonial world.

Americans, however, were totally neutral toward Vietnam with no material or emotional interest in it. Unhampered as they were by such factors, their involvement might have been rationally calculated within the framework of a global strategy. Was Vietnam a good place to halt the communist advance? Was it possible—and useful—to fight there especially in view of the moral implications? The French experience showed most emphatically that the answer had to be no. But Americans brushed that lesson aside without looking farther into it: they figured out that the French had lost first because they were colonialists—and *eo ipso* immoral—and second because they did not know how to wage a modern war.

There was a double lapse of intelligence: arrogance on the part of the Washington establishment and complete ignorance of the country on the part of the local commanders. Just after World War II the United States had the best means ever available to gather information and knowledge in the countries it had fought against. This explains the success of the Marshall Plan and of the occupation of Japan which were masterpieces of wisdom even more than of generosity. But only fifteen years later, generals, diplomats, and politicians had given up reasoning except in abstractions. Nobody ever took the time to study the terrain and the human context seriously. Programs had to be good in the abstract because of their intrinsic logic and their public relations impact. This means for all practical purposes the reign of the bureaucracy in its worst form. And such seems still to be the case if we are to judge from American policy in Africa, in the Middle East, in Iran, or now in Central America.

Failures and dramas usually do not come alone. Lapse of intelligence here is a social phenomenon that will entail the same errors in other kinds of activities. Vietnam was the touchstone of the American crisis. But the crisis was much deeper than Vietnam. It was the roots, not the consequence, of that war. Rationality was to suffer as much in domestic as in foreign politics during these years of confusion in Washington, D.C. Lyndon Johnson lost on the domestic side as much and as well as he lost in Vietnam. Waging the war on poverty just when he was waging a war in Vietnam was already an impossible risk. But his war on poverty was as ill conceived as the war against the Vietcong. That he could not succeed when saddling the budget, the economy, and society as a whole with burdens impossible to bear and claims impossible to answer cannot be explained away by the cost of Vietnam. It bore witness to the same megalomaniac sense of abundance and suffered from the same incapacity to accept the limits of human endeavors and the implied necessity of making choices and of working through a seriously thought-out strategy. Was it Johnson's fault alone? Was it not a collective delusion on the part of the whole American society?

One does not solve problems, as Ted Kennedy and some of his Democratic colleagues were to discover many years later, by throwing millions of dollars at them. One does not transform society by improving legal provisions and ordering well-meaning bureaucrats to oversee their implementation. One does not right the wrongs done to the black community during several generations by having the children of the present generation, black and white, pay the full price of ill-conceived abstract busing plans. One does not decide so lightly about affirmative action legal procedures without paying attention to their consequences. To do so has been only to exacerbate tensions, degrade institutions, and finally produce an irresistible backlash.

The whole Western world to be sure was caught up at this time in the same deep moral crisis. But contrary to all traditional expectations, the strongest country, the richest, the one with the most leeway and the best tradition to adjust quickly to any circumstances and meet any challenge, the USA, was hit the hardest. For almost an entire decade, the land of consensus turned into the land of disorder and tumult. The crisis was first experienced as a confluence of local revolts; blacks, students, women, minorities of all kinds. But it quickly became apparent that these revolts, instead of drawing up specific demands

71

and evolving into the traditional game of negotiation and compromise, crystallized into a truly religious movement in which each particular struggle seemed to grow out of a single sacred cause.

The American moral crisis more than any other took on an almost metaphysical dimension that blocked off the sight of reality and created the desperate feeling of being caught in a blind alley. The situation of the blacks and the war in Vietnam were no longer concrete problems that had to be worked on and gradually improved if not solved but instead were Evil Incarnate saturating the fabric of everyday life. Since every authority, not just the federal government but all authorities public and private, proved unable to respond to requests that were both excessive and contradictory, the crisis shattered the consensus and the fabric of social relationships.

According to everyday logic, the more people interact the better they get along, make compromises, come to understand one another, and settle their conflicts. But there is also a logic of disorder according to which the more contacts people have, the more they detest one another and the more they demand, protest, and attack without provocation; the more conflicts feed on themselves; this is the logic of escalation.

Western political theory is based on the first model but Western practice has always been very much influenced by the fear of the second. Bulwarks of authority, distance, and secrecy have protected those in charge of maintaining peace and leading the commonwealth. For the first time since the emergence of the modern democratic state at the end of the eighteenth century, these bulwarks have been called into question. Americans who had believed more than the citizens of any other Western nation in the sacred nature of their institutions were more deeply hurt.

They found, it seems to me, another Shakespearean hero to use as a major scapegoat: Richard Nixon, King Richard, the prince of liars, who provoked the nation at its very heart.

Nixon was an accident but also the product of his time and circumstances. And Watergate was not just his problem. It also expressed some of the basic problems of present-day American culture. Watergate simply cannot be understood in any other way. It is impressive to discover that no other contemporary event has provoked so much transatlantic misunderstanding, or should I say disagreement. Americans would be wise not to dismiss as lightly as they usually do European comments about Watergate. Not because these comments are right but because, whatever their naiveté, reading them seriously would help Americans gain a distance that is for them as indispensable as it is difficult.

As everybody knows, Europeans point out the disproportion between the third-rate burglary episode of Watergate and the dramatic consequences of forcing a president to resign and paralyzing the country at a historical moment fraught with difficulties. Such shabby business may have revealed the deplorable moral standards of some of the people on the Nixon staff, but no one implied that it had any impact at all on the 1972 election. Why could not it be dealt with without jeopardizing the overriding interests of the state and the stability of international relations?

Some of my American friends remind me at that stage of the Dreyfus affair. True enough, there is some similarity. Yet the issues were different in 1900 France. A man's life and honor were truly at stake. And anti-Semitism was definitely a major moral and political issue.

What was at stake with Watergate it seems to me was of a completely different nature. Nixon's behavior was incredibly shocking to the country's self-image and therefore unacceptable for a president. What counted was not the facts of the case but the behavioral pattern underlying them. Nixon was cheating and refused to respect the law which it was his mission to uphold. What Europeans cannot understand is why cheating poses so basic a problem to the American people. I would submit that it is because cheating is the only behavior that will break the system of trust that supports America's institutions and its characteristic network of human relations.

The postulate of trust in one's fellows makes everything infinitely easier in American society. All things are simple in so virtuous a democracy, except that one is all the more vulnerable to evil since one refuses to acknowledge its existence. And evil keeps on raising its ugly head. It always takes the form of cheating, which is enough to shatter the bond of trust and imperil the whole community; but at the same time cheating is a very common practice. A society built on trust naturally gives rise to many opportunities for cheating and makes that act both easy and lucrative. The extraordinary reaction of the American public to the scandal of Charles Van Doren cheating on the quiz show is a good example of the tremendous importance trust has in the country.

Thus Nixon could be looked upon as a scapegoat, someone who embodies the dark side of American consciousness, a world teeming with suspicion, lies, and extortions. One finds this world well portrayed in hundreds of detective stories where corrupt judges and crooked cops, the pawns of gangsters and politicians, are uncovered by a private detective or a fighting District Attorney. Robert Woodward and Carl Bernstein fit that tradition admirably, their exploits recalling Humphrey Bogart at his finest.

But why Nixon, why just at this time? After all, other politicians had been caught before and were caught thereafter cheating. One can only speculate about it. But scapegoating is an ancient and ever new ritual that humans collectively use when they feel their institutions and sacred beliefs are at stake. The questioning now should no longer be about Nixon's guilt but about what was at stake.

Some Further Questioning

Close as they still are to us, America's happy days of the fifties and sixties have now come to seem all but incomprehensible. Like a gigantic social landslide sundering continuity with the past, the Vietnam War has swept them far away. Photographs from that era have not yet faded, but already its cordial feelings, its splendid visions, its pious rhetoric and sweet sentimentality strike us as coming from another era.

Such happy days will not come back because the dream of them is a dream about lost innocence. America as a nation was blessed by keeping it alive much longer. But there is no New World/Old World opposition anymore. Innocence is out of reach for adult nations as much as for adult human beings.

Battered by failure and defeat, stunned by the way tragedy burst into the peaceable rounds of everyday life, thrown headlong into a history gone out of control, the country now tries to forget. It still mourns and clings to its lost illusions.

Something deeper corrodes its will, a problem it does not want to face and yet needs to face: Why did it happen? The question does not seek after the responsibility and guilt of individuals or groups nor political or ideological scapegoats; it seeks after the patterns and mechanisms that were involved. American ways were always supposed to be the best ones, the most efficient, the most democratic, the closest to justice. What went wrong? How could it happen that with all the goodwill in the world, the American people brought about so much evil?

What is really at stake is America's cherished traditional patterns and values, its image of itself. Not that it should discard its identity, but it may have to rethink and readjust it. It may have to learn. If one looks at all the major developed nations—Germany, Italy, France, Japan—they all learned a great deal from their failures and changed a great deal while rediscovering in their past the way to reassert a stronger identity. England, which did not suffer the same traumas, did not go as deeply in that search, and its long decline in these postwar years can be attributed surely to its incapacity to call itself into question.

This is now the time for America to learn again, to forget its dreams of innocence and superiority, to become humble enough to accept that there are lessons to learn from the rest of the world and from the facts. But in order to do that a nation must first be ready to work harder in understanding its own ways.

When one reviews the new intellectual reawakening that is so promising as a change of mood, one is struck by its very shyness in that respect. There is still too often a narrow technocratic bent to its solutions. This is especially true for economic and business affairs but also for education matters. The diagnoses are challenging but they seem to stop halfway. The diagnostician is so eager to get to practical solutions that he jumps to his own conclusions. This is not pragmatism. This is just lack of perspective and lack of realism.

To have a more fruitful search for answers to American problems, one simply must go beyond these sectional diagnoses to a more reasonable view of the system as a whole, of its trends, and of its capacities to react to new policies. True, action has to insert itself into technical domains, and it will use technical means. But it will succeed only if in the process of reasoning about the alternatives one takes seriously into account the context in which the action is going to take place. This context is not a void but a social system that has its own ways, its capacities to act and innovate by itself, and—just as important—a tremendous capacity to resist any government actions. Actions, programs, reforms have a chance to succeed only if they manage to help the system open up and learn. They may be sound technically and launched with the best intentions, but they will fail if they make the system regress.

If Americans want to restore their capacity to act efficiently and justly, they must therefore first come to understand what is the trouble with their system of action as a system. To this we now turn.

PART

II

THE TROUBLE
WITH AMERICA

*The fault, dear Brutus,
is not in our stars, but
in ourselves . . .*
—Shakespeare

CHAPTER FIVE

THE FEAR OF DECISION

**The Return of
Tragedy Sweeps
Away Illusions**

A N EXTRAORDINARY BOND linked the illusion of unlimited social progress (guarantee the freedom of all parties concerned and leave the rest to negotiation), the illusion of truth (unlock the answer to any problem with the key to knowledge), and the illusion of rationality (use applied science as the model for rational, efficient action). This perfectly coherent, optimistic, conceptual scheme seemed every bit as essential to humanity's forward progress as had older ideological systems in their day—critical reason in the eighteenth century, positivism at the end of the nineteenth. But unlike those elitist creeds, this one was held by the whole population, who in one way or another adhered to the postulates of trust in other people, faith in the virtues of consensus, and reverence for the rule of law; and so its power was immense. Americans could believe that the circle had been squared: progress would go on forever. It resembled the blissful end of history that Marxists still dream of.

But history returns to take its vengeance. The return of the tragic dimension was a reminder of death, the primordial and impassible barrier that stamps human life with the seal of irreversible time. Twenty wrongheaded years are now on the books, part of a history whose burden the country does not know how to shrug off. The world has changed tremendously. And wisdom bids us adapt to the reality of the present. But to adapt, one should change oneself deeply enough. The only question is how.

History abounds with instances of groups, categories, castes, and nations that failed to adapt and then sank into decline and oblivion. Every society faces the problem of managing to govern itself and to adjust its patterns of action to the changing conditions of the developing environment. Resolving this problem calls for a rejection of simplistic causal notions of history. Far from serving purely to assign responsibility or to determine the consequences of an event, history also reveals the weaknesses of any given system. For any model of action and its basic presuppositions, the crises of history are the decisive test. And to draw the right conclusions from such a test means to rethink the relevance of the model, judging from the results obtained. This is in no sense an attempt to make history over but to understand the observed mechanisms of repeated error and the confusions they have wrought.

Three major levels should be distinguished here: first, decision or politics in the broadest sense: why and how decisions are reached, for good or ill, on matters affecting the nation and the various collectivities within it; second, organization: the kinds of human relationships that predominate in public and private institutions, the types of apparatus used for resolving conflicts; and, finally, the level of philosophy, as it might be called, or ethics: the ideal image individuals have of good and evil and of life with their fellows.

The logical place to begin would be with the final—and main—point: the individual and his or her philosophy and moral vision. But this level, though the most profound and the one that controls the other two, is also the most obscure and conjectural. To comprehend it requires an understanding of the systems of decision and organization.

Failure of the American Form of Government

Nothing is more sacred to Americans than their form of government. The Declaration of Independence and the Constitution, with its separation of powers, are as dear to them as their celebrated way of life. The foreign visitor to Washington is overwhelmed by a sense of the sacred, much more potent there than in any other world capital. What is sacred is not so much the institutions themselves as the principles behind them, and not so much the substance of these principles as their very existence—the fact that they are beyond criticism or debate. The only problems they create are juridical and concerned strictly with implementation. This permanent framework enclosing the American political system is marvelously reassuring. It provides absolute stability—practically speaking, eternity.

In this context the sentiments of disgust and rejection one notices almost everywhere today seem altogether scandalous. This is much more than the traditional recriminations uttered by passionate reformers who indiscriminately lump together Democrats and Republicans. What we are seeing is a fundamental alienation of young people from political life, a deep lack of faith in institutions—as repeatedly shown by opinion polls—and declining participation in civic life. In many if not most elections less than half of the potential voters cast a ballot. In massive numbers Americans are now refusing to register, in the traditional manner, as Democrats or Republicans. For some years now the leading party in America has been the one made up of independents.

Everyone joins the chorus of complaints that the real issues are not being raised and that no leader worthy of the name has come out of the political process. Americans do not understand that their own political behavior is stifling the system. The critical issues are disappearing beneath an avalanche of demands from all the special interest groups, and no leader could ever accede responsibly to all their contradictory pressures. In this situation principles become rhetoric pure and simple, and respect for law turns into demagogy.

At this point we may stand back a bit from the American scene: decision-making systems are going through a crisis in *all* modern societies, owing precisely to the manifold success (and the resulting transformations) these societies have experienced. We see here two absolutely irresistible trends at work: on the one hand, the constantly increasing complexity of human relationships, which derives as a matter of course from technological progress, from the developing structures of exchange and interaction, from the ever broader access gained by all kinds of groups to the debate over issues concerning them. On the other hand, we note the accompanying growth of freedom for all citizens, both as economic agents and as actors on the political and social stage. Along with this irresistible movement toward complexity and freedom comes the communications revolution, abolishing time and distance, making it highly difficult to keep the decision-making process secret. No process can encounter such tremendous pressure without undergoing profound transformations. Hence it is necessary to find different modes of regulation to keep that pressure down.

For a long time I believed that since Americans had entered upon this evolution sooner than the rest of us, they would be the first to come up with practical new adaptations to it. This seemed all the more likely since they had more resources than anyone, since their geographical situation made them much less vulnerable than Europeans, and since they had hitherto shown more freedom of action and capacity for innovation than people anywhere else. But in reality that freedom and capacity had been maintained only within the framework of a fixed system. And once that system ran up against its own inherent limits, it proved unable to renew itself, and it plunged into a crisis.

That, in my opinion, is what we are seeing today. The problem may be a very old one, but it has not speeded up the discovery of solutions. Quite the contrary, its chronic status, exacerbated by the abrupt return of tragedy, has brought on an accelerated cycle of decline and panic. The decision-making process has become terribly complicated. When every group has access, one way or another, to every decision, one should not be surprised that the upshot is confusion and erratic choices. When everybody is free to go in and out everywhere without shouldering the least responsibility in return, when there is no social or cultural barrier to straighten out the chaos of negotiations, long-term policies are no longer feasible.

The major principles of the American system however seemed well suited to an already high level of complexity, so one thought they could easily adjust to new pressures. In the economic sphere nobody doubted that the law of supply and demand would always give rise to the best possible arrangement, as long as people respected due process. The laws of a free market and due process also applied, as we have seen, to the system of political decision making. Balancing all the various interests should naturally promote the public good, together with an optimally efficient market. To be sure, in the area of public decisions the problem of rationality still remained. But Americans cherished a mystical faith in the eventual convergence of technocratic rationality (based on scientific calculations) and political rationality (based on compromise and adjustment). Unfortunately, when the going gets too difficult, when complexity increases and gets out of hand, the long term vanishes behind the shrunken horizon of the present, and along with it goes any real opportunity for change and development. By now it is clear that if the system managed to stay more or less intact, it was because it was undergirded by something altogether different from principles.

There were, in fact, still powerful social and cultural structures sustaining and directing the flow of market activity. A certain feeling for the common good, as embodied in moral and civic authorities, marked off the bounds of what was negotiable among the various conflicting interests. Still more universal was the special notion of time: the country could always put off due dates, could always wait for favorable moments.

When social barriers collapse, broken down, by ease of access to decision making and the freedom of all concerned to follow their own paths to the bitter end, the rule of law becomes harder and harder to impose. Adjustments continue to be made, of course, but their pace keeps slackening, as the system closes in upon itself. The short term gradually absorbs the long term, there is no longer the time or the freedom needed to reflect and invest for the future.

And once the long term ceases to be adequately represented, it pays for each player in the political game to press his short-term demands to the limit. With much more latitude than he ever enjoyed before, the individual (or group) now has the luxury of displaying a fine intransigence. Thus, adjustments become more difficult, and they no longer contain the elements of flexibility and risk taking that once provided a way out of the zero-sum game dilemma (where it makes no sense for anyone to take the chance of collaborating with another person, since A's gain is B's loss).

Even the spread of knowledge ends up being counterproductive. Unmediated information overwhelms the public; there are snapshots but no perspective to put them into. Interests are engulfed by images, even short-term calculations are swept aside by the machinery of public relations. This downward spiral goes into high gear as soon as debate over long-term issues is dominated by the rhetoric of good and evil instant satisfaction, and when the short term is identified with the affective image that individuals and groups have of their moral and material interests. Under these circumstances man the political animal finds himself torn between a demagoguery that is forever harping on the grand old principles (so that even respect for the Constitution winds up as a tool for demagogues) and a cynicism that manipulates the interests and passions of the electorate.

The only way to break out of this spiral is to make everyone caught up in it renounce both idealism and cynicism, attitudes that both caricature and complement each other. And the only hope of getting around them lies in a return to the most hard-nosed realism. This implies a considerable effort on the part of Americans, who will have to show more tolerance on the level of abstract principle, more skepticism about the intrinsic capacities of government, and more willingness to take part in it. Paradoxically, the citizens of Europe, including the French, who look so skeptically on the powers of government and the virtue of governors, are in a better position to keep up their participation in the political process and to continue viewing it with tolerance. Americans used to seem much more capable of generosity than Europeans, but they are less resistant to the stresses and strains of political life. Their former naiveté makes them all the more vulnerable now to cynicism or alienation.

It may well be deplorable, but the basic fact remains that one cannot have democracy and decentralization without structures, and one cannot have structures without a minimum amount of tolerance for inequality and injustice.

The Decline of Traditional Structures

Up till recently the indispensable structures of this young country had been guaranteed by the respect paid both to the rights of its various communities and to historical and cultural privileges. The United States was a country made up of extremely vigorous communities. From their earliest years children had a sense of collective values inculcated in them at school. There were countless groups and associations. Boys and girls joined the Scouts as a matter of course, women were the driving force behind civic movements, and men could scarcely have a career unless they belonged to fraternal organizations. The past tense is crucial here, because if the immense network of associations has survived, it has also lost much of its vigor and undergone essential changes.

The schools, which in their own way represented living communities to which parents were strongly committed, have in many cases turned into battlegrounds. Often deserted by upper-middle-income families, they now suffer from a lack of leadership; the private schools can hardly function as beacons of democracy. Saluting the flag and reciting patriotic prayers have become ridiculous. The younger generations find the regimented style of scouting repugnant. Civic movements, PTAs, and all other groups based on volunteer activity have tended to languish in the wake of women's liberation: when women are working and fighting for their rights, they have other things to do besides running old-fashioned "ladies auxiliary" activities. The latter have now given way to associations for advancing or defending some common interest. These activities, to be sure, are distinctly alive and they encourage participation—but a somewhat negative kind of participation, so that they no longer make the same contribution to the support and development of the community. The social bond that once enabled people to make constructive compromises as well as to accept the sacrifices needed for the long run is coming undone. On a related issue it looks as if confrontation and litigation are on the rise. America is becoming a society caught up in a continual civil war. The schools are frequently the object of this struggle, but so, increasingly, are all community enterprises, and critics freely accuse them of favoritism and discrimination.

The rage for equality that worried Tocqueville a hundred and fifty years ago has progressively weakened the social fabric, to the point where the marvelous American capacity for association, which he once found so admirable, has been drained of its revitalizing power. The United States today is no longer the America Tocqueville described. Its voluntary associations have ceased to be the mainstay of a democracy constantly on the move but are now simply a means of self-defense for various interests (which, though perfectly ethical, are still parochial in nature). This breakdown of community structures is what has made America a country full of anxiety, and periodically shaken by reactionary crusades.

Sometimes too we see the old violent forms of community pressure return, more poisonous than ever. The United States has always been the land of moral order, as enforced especially by groups safeguarding public virtue. The pressure that Puritan communities exerted on their members bordered on the unbearable, leading many people to head off for more open and tolerant places. Thus, the colonization of the West owed at least in part to the energy of rebels and individualists. But the traditions and constraints of home had scarcely been left behind when the danger and solitude of the frontier created new ones, only cruder and hence much more violent. The epic journeys by covered wagon were also an ordeal of forced solidarity and intolerance. Lynching was just as common in the West as in the South, not racist hangings but executions of criminals and sometimes of mere deviants. By the end of the seventies America was in the grip of moral insecurity and began to spawn new vigilante associations, well-organized defenders of Law and Order. This movement has grown up around evangelical religious sects; its power, though short-lived and purely reactive, is awesome. It has helped to make adjustments even more difficult for a democracy that is already too complex and impersonal to function properly.

America's historical and cultural heritage gave rise to structures of a different sort, narrower but firmly in control of the decision-making process. The much-criticized WASPs used to constitute the power elite of the country. White Anglo-Saxon Protestants were the dominant force in all economic, social, and cultural activities. The nation had been shaped by their traditions, their customs, their moral concepts. The melting pot was open wide to the newcomers, but only if they were willing to accept the WASP model and their natural hegemony. No majority group—and the WASPs were very nearly that—ever makes up an elite all by itself. But the acknowledged superiority of this tradition and the hierarchical social order deriving from it guaranteed that the permanent (and relatively open) elites that incarnated its values would survive and be accepted. This kind of leadership was marked by a civic sense, a respect for moral duty, and a devotion to the community that spread naturally through the whole fabric of society. Without this solid framework the liberal, egalitarian American system could not have achieved the stability it did.

These elites, the repository of traditional values, were the guardians of both the political and the economic world. They held, almost by right, the high positions in Wall Street and the federal administration, in corporations and universities. Among the major WASP prerogatives, patronage of the arts ranked especially high. It was at the same time a way to whitewash fortunes made a bit too quickly and a sacrifice in honor of sacrosanct values, the symbolic stamp of noblesse oblige, imposing discipline and restraint, that is, limits to the struggle for power and money.

The accelerated evolution of American society brought on, among other things, the breakup of the WASP system and a weakening of the influence its values once had on the country's leaders. Without even realizing it, society has shed this anachronistic ball and chain; but it has also lost the sense of leadership and continuity that tradition had kept alive. In the fifties it looked as if the Jews would bring the WASP system the new energy it needed to go on. There was a convergence between the extraordinary boom in higher education, whose influence on public life grew apace, and the spectacular intellectual successes of young Jews. A leadership based on intelligence began to replace the traditional moral and social leadership, and the Kennedy presidency seemed bound to open the way for a Jewish-WASP fusion. But the Kennedy style did not have the time to impose itself. Besides, politics as public theater had already begun to get the upper hand over statesmanship, glamor was winning out over ethics. When Nelson Rockefeller in 1960 decided to marry the woman he loved, at the risk of hurting his chances of becoming president, he was still operating within the old chivalrous tradition of duty. But when John F. Kennedy was reconciled with his wife in order, so the story goes, to improve his image with the voters, an essential feature began to fade from public life. The fusion of Jewish and WASP elites took place after all, but the values that both groups incarnated had already been too badly eroded to halt the return of tragedy. The glamor of the Kennedy style was seductive but much more dangerous than the traditional WASP style, with its reserve and austerity.

The Vietnam War led to the bankruptcy of both models, the old and the new. The army, once the repository of traditional values (those of the WASPs, more precisely of southern WASPs) has now lost all its moral influence. It is no longer the army of General George Marshall and Dwight Eisenhower but an army of callous bureaucrats. The administrative elites have lost their prestige and faith in their mission. The old senators from the South, who were the congressional embodiment of continuity in public affairs, have been swept away by racial upheavals. The former oligarchs of Wall Street and the business world have seen their influence weaken in a system too complex, fast moving, and confused to be mastered. During the winter of 1968 some leaders of the WASP business establishment got together, at the request of Secretary of Defense Clark Clifford, to inform President Johnson that the business and financial community demanded an immediate end to that absurd war, but their decision to intervene came too late and went for nought. In an earlier day high-placed WASPs had managed to put an end to Joseph McCarthy's insane witch-hunt. The Vietnam War showed the limits of their influence.

The evolution of American politics has been gradually putting distance between these elites and political power. This might seem part of the normal workings of democracy, but it becomes dangerous when along with the elites the values of continuity that they represented begin to fade away. No society can afford to deny a leading role to long-term thinking. Of course, it is not necessary that a king, for example, should be the embodiment of continuity, but this function must be carried out by political—or, failing that, social—institutions. If society will no longer tolerate elites and political institutions do not provide the necessary safeguards for long-term planning, for the preparation that it implies, as well as for the risks, then democracy falls apart, both at the bottom, where the sense of community is lost, and at the top, where feeling for the state as a whole and the common good likewise suffers. A system of government may flatter its citizens by modeling itself on their passions, but it will all be in vain because they will increasingly reject any system lacking leadership—without which a community has no meaning.

When the Short Term Absorbs the Long Term

To understand the importance of the decline of elites at the top and of community leadership at the bottom, we must realize that the relations between long term and short term, between politics and administration, are totally different in the United States from their European counterparts. In Europe the long term is controlled in one way or another by the specialized organs of government, which are generally imbued with a special sort of ideology, a veritable mystique of the state, of administration, or at least of public service,[1] an ideology whose guardians are the castes of high-level, carefully screened officials. Such a system creates many dangers. The more or less spontaneous adjustment of conflicting interests can get swamped by completely unrealistic long-term theorizing. These castes also have their own partisan interests and professional biases. Narrow and monopolistic, they easily become hidebound, owing to the lack of competition, both from within and without.

In the United States the problem is exactly the reverse: institutions or castes specializing in the long term simply do not exist. Americans trust that if the short term is handled alertly enough the long term will take care of itself. More precisely, there are two implicit assumptions governing the conduct of public affairs:

1. The free-market exchange of goods, services, and jobs—and, beyond that, of information, culture, ideas, and even of public goods— always brings about the best possible arrangement for the nation as a whole.

2. This market gives rise automatically and incrementally to the reforms it needs to function properly.

Judging from experience, the first assumption seems legitimate. To be sure, it demands inventiveness in a certain number of borderline cases, especially when dealing with public goods, but it always makes for an excellent starting point. Unfortunately, this is by no means true

---

[1]The Germans have gotten rid of the traditional Prussian bureaucracy, but the mystique of the state still remains. In England the Parliament comes first, but civil servants working for the Treasury are the guardians of national continuity. So are the members of the "Grands Corp" in France.

of the second assumption. The best immediate adjustment does not necessarily lead to reform or even to the innovations needed for the system to progress. Like all human institutions, a market, even of the simple economic variety, is very liable to get ossified.

To appreciate the truth of this, consider the following example from the world of business: the use of computers in managing a company allows a much clearer view of its performance and, above all, it puts such information in the hands of executives more quickly than before. At first it was thought that this higher degree of clarity would make competition fairer and so enable decision makers to approach an optimum level of efficiency, but we see that it has quite often helped to make them more cautious and conservative. When financial analysts receive reports on their company's overall performance at the end of every quarter, they find themselves constrained to keep their day-to-day operations under increasingly narrow surveillance, at the risk of losing their reputation on the financial markets—that implacable judge of the managerial profession.

This fear heightens the importance of quantitative, short-term management, as opposed to the necessarily qualitative preparation called for by the long term. More generally speaking, the sharper the competition, the less willing competitors will be to try uncertain innovations. Nobody wants to risk the chances he has. Many management specialists are beginning to be troubled by this phenomenon. They wonder if the rationalization they promoted so energetically has not had, when all is said and done, a stifling effect. When accountants, economists, and lawyers replace technicians and entrepreneurs, the system loses its productivity.[2] The reader will doubtlessly object that foreign competition will force American business to make changes. A perfectly valid point, but no changes will take place unless some oppressive aspects of this "transparent" market are done away with. Furthermore, American business is facing competition, paradoxically enough, from the Japanese, who operate under quite different assumptions. The free market, in fact, does not facilitate innovation except within certain limits. Unless constantly reoriented, it can become an immobilizing force. Five or six Mozarts are assassinated every day, someone said, by way of criticizing the social and economic barriers to the free development of talent. But those geniuses could just as easily be trampled under foot by an undisciplined democratic mob. Innovation is impossible without the time and freedom which only a certain elitism can guarantee. In many cases the immediate adjustment

[2]The point has been made forcefully by Robert Reich, *The Next American Frontier.*

of conflicting interests adds up to success for mediocrities, who form a coalition against their betters.

Of course, all this is even more true of political decisions, because the problem of the long term is constantly present in the public sector, and if the assumption of incrementalism falls short, the system will not be viable. One might retort that this assumption, all things considered, has worked pretty well, but this is attributable to a number of causes: the American system, with its enormous human and material resources, could live with much more waste than could European systems; hence there was less need for government. With less tension among the various interest groups, the leadership provided by the traditional cadres and the institutions created by them was sufficient. Since the country's elites were capable of attending to its long-term needs, America was not bothered by a state that invaded the private lives of its citizens. And its extreme decentralization, grounded in the vigor of local communities, made things still easier: cultural institutions, foundations, universities (often run by those same elites) gradually took on more responsibility as the pace of public life quickened.

But the postwar period witnessed a tremendous increase in this burden, at the very moment when the decline of the old elites dramatically weakened their capacity to handle it. The Johnson presidency seems to have been the breaking point: from then on the system got out of control and has shown itself less and less governable. The long term is increasingly swallowed up by the short term, which is itself swallowed up by public relations. The tendencies to drift, which were always there, have undergone a brutal acceleration. First of all there is the drift in purpose on the part of Congress, which is primarily concerned with the best way to adjust political interests (= how to be reelected). Thus, any legislative measure will be the result of a short-term adjustment of those interests, rather than of long-term reflection on the needs of the body politic and its capacities for growth, training, and transformation.

Corresponding to this drift in purpose is the drift in application and enforcement: the federal bureaucracy, which has to carry out the inadequate legislation handed it by Congress, becomes locked in the task of defending its own interests and the doctrine justifying them, and so it stops encouraging the free circulation of information. The widening gap between theory and practice alienates both sectors, while their interconnection, which is much stronger than in Europe, leads them to reach an understanding on their respective interests rather than on preparations for the future. The individual congressman wants to secure benefits for his district so as to win over his constituents. The federal bureaucrat insists that his programs be enlarged or at least preserved. The runaway expansion of the federal apparatus has turned the executive branch, which in America simply means the presidency, into another machine for short-term transfers of political credit. The country is getting closer and closer to a public relations dictatorship. The hyperactive and anxious Carter presidency was in many respects a reign of appearances where the only thing that mattered was the image in the public's eye. Ronald Reagan's presidency may be as calm and cheerful as the Carter one was agitated and anxious; its main preoccupation nevertheless is still with appearances.

Naturally people keep on talking about the long term, but in the kingdom of appearances it is just conventional moralizing. Every president, every politician is anxious for the approval of his conscience. And presidents have the right, when they leave office, to take their archives with them and to set up a foundation that will assure that the memory of their good conscience remains fresh.

The Problem of Information

The problem of information is growing more and more crucial in all complex social groups, and it is absolutely decisive for the functioning of democracy. Access to information for all citizens is an indispensable condition of modern democratic life, but it is a very onerous condition, because the least shift in the flow of information can warp the whole texture of democracy. On the subject of information, Americans follow an assumption just like the ones they accept concerning politics and the market. They think it goes without saying that if all the obstacles to freedom and aboveboard exchange of information were done away with, the best possible information would emerge. They refuse to recognize the fact that information often follows Gresham's law: the bad sort chases out the good. Without a doubt freedom is indispensable, but it is not enough. All relations with the public are complex and not limited to the immediate situation. Learning patterns develop, a certain leadership gets exercised, a responsibility comes into play, and it can be a heavy one.

But, more concretely, what is the origin of the problem as we know it today? Not so long ago there seemed to be only one imperative in this area: limit the pressure of financial interests on the press. Since the press, like all other industries, needed capital, the people who supplied it never failed to turn it to their own advantage. Public financing is not a very appealing alternative here, given the risk of monopolization or at least politicization. In the face of what for Europeans is a fundamental dilemma, Americans could see only one possible answer: free competition.

Well, the rapid changes of the last fifteen years have appreciably reduced the scope of the difficulty, even though management is again exerting heavy pressure on the news media. Journalists have in effect won a higher degree of independence. Their influence as a group, as a socioprofessional category with its own rules, norms, and special customs, now seems to carry more weight than financial interests that are no more in a position to enforce their dictatorial will.

In the final analysis the kind of relationship that journalists have with their public appears to be the determining factor. And this relationship tends to bring with it an increasing burden of distortions. If you want to move the public, you have to stress the human angle, the true-life details, the emotions. Thus, the encounter between the public and any medium of communication always has a moral slant to it. Television reinforces this bias: it thrusts aside complex explanations; the things it shows have to be registered quickly, with the maximum impact. As far as the press goes, "Find out who's guilty" is the only message that transcends the here and now, however slightly, and which journalism can treat at any length. In the spring of 1980 the highest Nielsen rating went to the made-for-TV movie about young lovers from Saudi Arabia executed by a cruel prince. Apart from the quality of the film, it clearly contributed nothing to the public's knowledge of the realities of life in the Mideast. On the contrary it muddied that knowledge by its "human" (i.e., emotional and superficial) treatment of what was supposedly an objective investigation.

In general, one gets the very distinct impression that in the United States today knowledge of foreign countries has steadily decreased. Some rudiments of political geography probably get through to the public, as crises strike one part of the globe after another, but this information is basically short term. The coverage of foreign news is much poorer today than it was thirty or even fifty years ago. In the good old days of Ernest Hemingway every self-respecting American newspaper had correspondents in the main capitals of Europe. They all used to write long background reports, and some of them developed a keen sense of the issues troubling the countries where they lived and in which they were deeply interested. In the fifties this expensive way of doing things began to be streamlined, and today the number of permanent correspondents has been drastically reduced. Information is attended to no longer by on-site journalists but by experts based in New York who prepare files on various topics and by executants who answer their questions. If a crisis comes up, a team is dispatched to the spot to gather some "local color"—without any perspective to put it in. They are, after all, specialists in communications, not in the particular country or problem at issue. The information produced by this system has undeniably been checked out and its gaps have been filled; it stands a better chance of getting the details right. But it also takes a heavier risk of neglecting overall quality and everything else that may help readers acquire some essential education on their own.

For all democracies, and particularly for the United States today, information is ultimately much more than just information: it involves a critical responsibility for the orientation of society at large. Despite the importance of the media in America and their quality, Americans are unquestionably underinformed and misinformed—a fact which may surprise some people but which in any case raises serious difficulties. Seven years after the Yom Kippur war, half the people in America still did not believe that their country imported oil. This extraordinary figure explains to a large extent their reactions to the energy crisis. And, given such ignorance, the media cannot be wholly absolved of guilt. At times their message may not have gotten through, but that only goes to show that the system has drifted off into trivia, appearances, and spectacular immediacy. Journalists are victims of this system, of course, but they are also partly responsible for it. In any case they are the ones whose job it would be to fix it.

Public opinion polls add to the distortion to the extent that they always focus on the here and now, on feelings, while eliminating qualitative reflection in favor of quantifiable preferences. The question is: How are these trends to be reversed, how to give the information business a sense of responsibility. No regulations or legal constraints can do the job. But this is an area where the long term *must* be rehabilitated. Foundations ought to tackle the problem, and at least as much care should be expended on getting good information as on any other service.

Intellectual Decline

The more complex a society becomes, the more its survival depends upon intellectual creativity. A society that is still relatively traditional can maintain its equilibrium through respect for tradition. Since it does not question the existing order, it has no need to examine the meaning of that order. Continuity is inscribed in the very nature of things. By contrast a society that lives in and for the future has altogether different needs. Once it no longer believes in the intrinsic virtue of things as they are, and tradition can no longer serve it as a reliable guide, it absolutely must turn elsewhere to keep itself going. At this point intellectual creativity takes over this vital role, rescuing it from the short term and the hurly-burly of public opinion that the latter's reign provokes.

Just after World War II the United States seemed to have found an admirable solution to the problem. No modern society had ever faced the future with so deep a "reservoir of thought," so stocked an arsenal of talents, and so favorable a climate for deploying them. It appeared to be the first country that could enter the age of rationality without fear. But this was a pure illusion: what looked like a promising moment had come about only because of an extraordinary—and ephemeral—combination of circumstances. And the decline in intellectual creativity was destined to have results all the more dramatic in that Americans had gotten used to their good fortune.

Why did the strength of 1945 turn into the weakness of today? The paradox may appear incomprehensible, but it should not. America in the fifties profited from the falling off of a totally unprecedented war effort, which had mobilized the enthusiasm not just of the best brains in the country but in the entire world. Beyond that the United States had benefited from the massive emigration by scientists and intellectuals from Central Europe. The war, for them, was a moment of creative effervescence: America was a new nation, an open nation, with no baneful traditions that might have trammeled their efforts. The federal government, taught by the New Deal brain trusts to respect science and scientific research, could offer them practically inexhaustible resources. Then, too, the blend of different cultures and disciplines brought an immediate enrichment. This was a time of original finds and grandiose projects, not only for the natural sciences but also for the social sciences. Philosophers and mathematicians who had never thought about such things before were asked to "huddle" over the problem of security for convoys of ships. This led to the discovery of methods of operations research that would later prove highly lucrative in the business world. Never before had such intense labor been devoted to the study of different cultures, seen from the vantage of their reaction to the problems of the war. Modern social psychology and the comparative ethnology of developed countries saw the light of day with the war or took an enormous leap forward because of it. The extraordinary success of reconstruction in Japan was owing in large measure to this investment of mental energy: the experts who had worked on the war effort were ready for the occupation. Without that investment the Marshall Plan—and hence the reconstruction of Europe—would not have been possible.

How is it, then, that barely twenty years later one could already witness so drastic a decline? I have already pointed out that when the United States became involved in Vietnam, there were no longer any qualified American experts on the Far East. And even the lessons taught by the war itself were no longer available. Consider, for example, that the immense number of studies done on the effects of U.S. aerial bombardment—which showed overwhelmingly how pointless it was—were never put to use.

This breakdown can be explained by various clear-cut factors. In particular the witch-hunts of the McCarthy era had caused the gravest kind of damage. David Halberstam ably demonstrates how the combination of McCarthyism and the Cold War, which had turned Communist China into the epitome of evil, ultimately led to the elimination of all independent thought in this area.[3] It was neglected, passed over; most of the leading lights backed away from it; and policy became more and more purely routine. Nevertheless, with the end of the fifties and the election of President Kennedy there was a spectacular revival, if not in the field of Far Eastern affairs, at least in the intellectual establishment as a whole. Sputnik had sent out shock waves that touched every bearer of intellectual and moral authority in America. There was a mighty campaign, launched and orchestrated by the WASP establishment (perhaps its last successful initiative), which led to the upgrading of science in the high schools, to a spectacular increase in expenditures for research, to a rejuvenation of the universities. The Ford Foundation and other like organizations spent millions of dollars to get the best minds back into research by generously supplementing the salaries of people whose leadership seemed essential.

But this reaction, for all its vigor, fell short. The enthusiasm and extraordinary drive of the war years was missing. The blend of talents was missing, as well as, perhaps, a certain kind of modesty: during the war years Americans had regarded the promises of science (still largely foreign to them) with reverence; in the sixties they were a bit too quick to assume that they already had those promises in hand. It may be that above all they were victims of the acceleration of history, which induced them both to look for growth (which was poorly understood in the first place) and to let themselves be engulfed by the short

[3]David Halberstam, *The Best and the Brightest* (New York: Random House, 1972).

term. In any event, the crisis of the early seventies arrived before the reforms in progress had come to fruition. The Vietnam War had deeply troubled the morale of the scientific community. The financial and employment crisis inevitably caused the system to solidify at a low level of efficiency. In the social sciences, as I tried to show earlier, a kind of reverse natural selection occurred. A final, and by no means insignificant, element has to be kept in mind: the years of sound and fury went a long way toward compromising the prestige of the universities and the intellectual establishment in the eyes of many Americans. Intellectual creativity was declining at the very moment when intellectuals found themselves being rejected by society as a whole.

The United States wound up being victims of their own colonialism. The French are wrong to complain about having to learn English. They would do better to rejoice, since people who do not have to learn foreign languages run a very high risk of drifting into arrogance and becoming trapped in their private world.

Recivilizing Politics

A political system bogged down in the short term and in public relations cannot give society the kind of direction it needs. The United States has gotten caught up in a vicious circle of indecision. It no longer has adequate leadership either for the country at large or for local communities, nor is there enough intellectual creativity to support the thinking absolutely indispensable for the long term. People consider social development only insofar as it relates, on the one hand, to the adjustment of conflicting interests and, on the other, to the application of moral and legal principles. Procedures, institutions, and regulatory mechanisms are all thought of as natural and untouchable—just when a national crisis is bringing all their shortcomings to light. The fact is that a highly adaptive, nonstop society does not have the time to examine the implications of all the little adjustments it makes on short notice. Distracted by the immediate hustle and bustle, it fails to see that from a broader perspective it is frozen in place.

For a long time the rising social status of the university community nourished hopes that a new elite was about to emerge. Daniel Bell spoke of a class of "theoreticians," while J. K. Galbraith has urged, more concretely, a new alliance among various groups of well-educated people. This "intellectual party" is the one that John Anderson (with a political orientation far different from Galbraith's) tried to reach in his 1980 presidential campaign. Again, this is the "party" that Gary Hart has tried to mobilize in 1984. But intellectuals may be as much the prisoners of the system, and maybe more so, than the rest of the electorate. The crucial problem, I believe, is more difficult and more profound: American politics has to be recivilized. This implies the introduction of new values, more complex than the simpleminded ethics that seems the order of the day in a populist world— the values of patience, respect, discretion, endurance. The turnabout calls for an immense educational effort so that the public can draw closer to the national elites and so that the elites can break out of their complacency, arrogance, and insularity.

CHAPTER SIX

THE DELIRIUM OF DUE PROCESS

IF THERE IS ONE BASIC STRUCtural principle governing all American life, it is not, as one might think, the scientific organization of labor or modern management techniques. Rather, it is a juridical principle: absolute respect for the rules of procedure. These rules, with their impersonal constraints, take precedence over all underlying problems, for they alone guarantee human freedom and the unimpeded pursuit of happiness. No Frenchman or any other European can ever really feel at home with the extraordinary juridical ideology with which the whole of American society is imbued, and which can be summed up in two words—due process.

To make this ideology more intelligible, I would like to begin by caricaturing it, at the risk of offending some readers. The point of departure for this American notion is that individuals are free, absolutely free, with no ifs, ands, or buts, to do exactly as they want. The only evaluation of their conduct that can be tolerated, the only criterion compatible with the affirmation of radical liberty, applies to the individual's relations with other people and with institutions, which emanate from the collectivity. Here or elsewhere, of course, there can be no question of prescribing to anyone what he or she should do. The individual is merely informed what procedures are to be followed so that any difficulties that might arise can be regulated.

The American approach, which outsiders so often find shocking in specific cases, starts out from the idea that it is up to the individual alone to decide what he wants to do; the procedures are there to counterbalance the dangers of individualism by preserving that vital element in all human relationships—trust. As with economic matters, here too the smooth functioning of the system as a whole rests entirely on the foundation of individual freedom. The "invisible hand" that accomplishes this miracle is precisely the trust people have in the system and the natural sense of respect linking them together. The role of the law goes no farther than safeguarding the permanence of that trust and respect, without otherwise interfering in the life of individuals who are busy pursuing happiness as they see fit—a notion written right at the beginning of the Declaration of Independence. Hence Americans never experience the typically European impulse of rebellious resistance toward the law, never having been, like the Europeans, constantly subject to the ancestral law of princes—a law that later became impersonal without losing any of its coercive character.

There is something admirable and touching about the awe Americans feel toward their Constitution, whose principles they internalize more thoroughly than any other nation in history. But it must be noted that this way of doing things has its disadvantages. For one, the reduction of law to a body of forms and procedures often falls short of what is actually needed: fear of the policeman, in America as everywhere else, is sadly indispensable for social order and morality. But, above all, this obligation of citizens to internalize the major principles of common life is a heavy burden for the individual and full of dangers for society, especially given the restraints weighing the latter down. The repressive puritanical ethos that long remained so potent in the small towns of the South and West frequently led to the worst excesses, such as lynching. The law of the prince, by contrast, oppressive and arbitrary, as it was in the past, has become gradually more tolerant and less demanding for the individual. It gives everyone the right to think as he pleases in his heart of hearts, without having to bear a terrible burden of guilt. What it takes away from freedom of action, it restores in freedom of thought; and many times the individual may well consider himself better off from the exchange.

On another issue, the law of the prince is on the whole much more efficient at fighting crime: the prince can readily and deliberately exercise his arbitrary power. Such law is open to abuse, as critics have rightly observed, but it amply makes up for this. American law, which is based on trust, would do wonders in a virtuous world. But its crucial flaw is that it protects crime and injustice along with virtue, providing the criminal agrees to play the complicated procedural game. Frank Browning and John Gerassi's expression "the American way of crime" goes too far, but one has to acknowledge the extraordinary opportunities that justice in the United States offers to wrongdoers and, on a larger scale, to all sorts of cheaters. It is no rare event for the law to protect the guilty party (with help from a good lawyer) and crush the innocent (should he be ever so slightly naive or inept).

The terrifying saga of the Mafia is doubtless too artistically neat to be true. But if organized crime is not the perfectly oiled machine that films and novels make it out to be, it nonetheless occupies a very considerable place in American society.

Speaking at Harvard in 1978 Solzhenitsyn remarked: "Yet strangely enough, though the best social conditions have been achieved in the West, there still remains a great deal of crime, there even is considerably more of it than in the destitute and lawless Soviet society."[1] Solzhenitsyn was right, but this is much truer of America than of Europe.

In contrasting America with Europe here, I am not trying to accuse one and justify the other. There are good and bad points on both sides. The American system, which has been too much idealized for lack of sufficient concrete analysis, *is* distinguished by a consistency and universality that are not without grandeur. But, apart from a certain powerlessness to defend itself from misuse for blameworthy or even criminal ends, it is vulnerable to moral and philosophical criticism in that its very principles make it function with a rigidity sometimes bordering on the inhuman. European, and particularly French, tradition put the king beyond the law. He might abuse this privilege, but then again he might also live up to popular expectations and use it to correct any law whose literal application, in a given case, would be unjust. France overthrew the monarchy but did not abolish privilege. I once spoke (in 1959) with the prefect of a French *département,* whose career would later take him to the very top, and who bluntly told me: "Sir, a prefect is there to break the law. If there was no need of breaking the law from time to time in order to protect the innocent or to assure the public welfare, there would be no need

---

[1]Alexander Solzhenitsyn, "A World Split Apart: The World Demands from Us a Spiritual Blaze" in *Vital Speeches of the Day* (1978), p. 678.

for prefects." Coming from an official specifically entrusted with the job of making people respect the law, this comment, even if strictly confidential, would strike Americans as utterly scandalous. Isn't that proof, if more were needed, of what bad citizens Europeans are? Notoriously indifferent to public affairs, they dodge all their civic duties and practice tax fraud as if it were an exciting sport. As a matter of fact, if the French have long paid less in taxes than Americans, it is because France still had a much higher proportion of certain very common professions (agriculture, handicrafts, small business) members of which could conceal their assets much more easily. Other things being equal, Americans cheat just as eagerly as the French, and are quite skilled at profiting from the intricacies of their tax laws, which are far more complex than ours. Besides, if they take the affairs of their local community much more seriously, Americans vote a lot less than the French. They also refuse, rather uncivilly, the duty of conscription, a debt Europeans have discharged with a constancy that will be the marvel of future generations.

Another characteristic of American law that ought to be pointed out is its unpitying harshness. Once the machine is set in motion, nothing stops it. It pursues its victims so obstinately and relentlessly one would think it thirsty for vengeance. I shall not cite the Rosenbergs as an example, since their case was too obviously political. But around the same time another affair made headlines in America and the world: Caryl Chessmann was accused of rape and condemned to death, but his lawyers managed to plead his cause in trial after trial for eleven years, trying every procedural resource in the book, only to see his execution finally take place. The evidence of his guilt was not that strong, a lot of time had passed, and meanwhile Chessmann had published a book that turned out to be a best-seller. Now, in France some sort of pardon would certainly have come through, but then Governor Pat Brown, though a liberal Catholic and opposed to the death penalty, did not dare to counter inexorable justice with what would have looked elsewhere nothing more than elementary humanity.

It is true that since then the decline of traditional social structures has had profound effects on the rule of law, but the same does not hold for the principle of due process, which has, in a way, become still more rigid and impersonal. Up till this stage the WASPs imposed a kind of morality that was surely puritanical but that, without putting itself above the law, helped to make it more flexible. They also spread about, by means of various organizations, the values of charity: a pharisaical charity, perhaps, but charity nonetheless. The decline of

WASP society and its spirit means, inter alia, the disappearance of the humanitarian sentiments once produced by that enormous good-works machine.[2]

Lastly, we have to realize how closely due process is connected to the assumption of trust: this is the fundamental compact on which rests the whole development, economic and otherwise, of American society. Whenever critics complained of injustices in the system, its defenders used to reply, first, that it contained a self-correcting mechanism which automatically sets right its (admittedly deplorable) imperfections; and, second, that in the long run the system was immensely productive, because it drove individuals to use all their resources and achieve a success that would in the end contribute to the common good. This aspect of due process plainly reveals the laissez-faire ideology that, as we saw earlier, is realistic, efficient—and dangerous. So long as this principle was counterbalanced by political and, most important, social structures, everything was fine. But nowadays those counterweights are tending more and more to disappear, and this just when another (and altogether decisive) transformation is making exclusive recourse to laissez-faire as ill suited to America's new situation as it has been for some time in Europe.

The American system, based on due process and the pursuit of individual happiness, was very well attuned to the context of the frontier and to unlimited economic development. In a society of this sort the most pressing need is to mobilize human resources, to spur on the spirit of enterprise and conquest. To this end the presumption of mutual trust creates the most powerful bond, and the principle of due process provides the most effective guarantee. Given the extraordinary results achieved, the flaws in the system, however regrettable, can be endured.

The moral crisis America is going through today grows out of the discovery that the limits to a development thought to be unlimited have now been reached. America is beginning to experience what some recent historians of the Middle Ages, Pierre Chaunu in particular, have called the "time of saturation" (*temps du monde plein*).[3] After three or four centuries of constant and totally anarchic development Europe entered, around the twelfth century, into a new era, the era

---

[2] All Western societies are undergoing the same evolution, but other forces can still partly counterbalance the harshness of the law.

[3] See Pierre Chaunu, *L'expansion européenne due XIIIeme au XVeme siècle* (Paris: Presses Universitaires de France, 1969), and especially Georges Duby, *The Early Growth of the European Economy: Warriors and Peasants from the Seventh to the Twelfth Century* (Ithaca: Cornell University Press, 1974).

of saturation, which lasted until the great expansionist and imperialist movements of the sixteenth century.

The old dream of the westward course of Empire, which never faded completely, was destined to find new life in America and to inspire the vision of the world which we have analyzed. Over the past three hundred years it has taken on a force and vitality that make it hard to shake, even though this is a sine qua non for the restoration of American society.

Legalism, American Style

Due process is not just an ideological substrate of American life; it expresses itself in a number of concrete practices and procedures, such as the disproportionate influence of lawyers and legal experts in every sphere of activity. In the United States there are, per capita, eight times as many lawyers as in France, twenty times as many as in Japan.[4] If public life in France is dominated by civil servants, and the business world by engineers, in America the legal profession reigns supreme. Under Carter eight of thirteen cabinet secretaries were lawyers. General counsels, whether of corporations or political administrations, are always eminent figures. Even labor unions have come to be heavily influenced by their attorneys, some of whom have actually become union leaders, flying in the face of rules requiring (as in many other countries) the election of workers from the trade in question. The royal road to a great career always passes through the prestigious East Coast law schools, most notably Harvard. (The hero of *Love Story*—blue blood, splendid prospects, the finest "catch" imaginable—naturally goes to Harvard Law.)

This legal hypertrophy, although it has recently picked up speed, is nothing new, and has its roots in the way the American system is organized. When liberty is absolute, it becomes, for this very reason, a source of danger, and protection from its possible effects becomes absolutely indispensable. As we see in many Westerns, the West was

---

[4]Figures are very difficult to compare because professional categories differ from country to country. In the last two or three years, many more references and statistics are available. Derek Bok, in his presidential report to the Harvard overseers, gave some striking statistics. See *The President's Report—1981–82* (the Harvard Corporation, 1983).

The *Los Angeles Times* in a series of articles, 12–20 February 1984, offered a thorough review of the subject. From 1960 to 1983, the number of lawyers has more than doubled from 250,000 to 622,000; in ratio to population it means going from 1 per 632 to 1 per 375. Projections for 1995 were 1,000,000 lawyers—1 per 260 (*Los Angeles Times*, 18 February 1984).

won not simply with six-guns but with legal documents. Sheriffs and marshals (all of them officers of the court) played a key role, and not very far behind them we see judges, lawyers, and politicians (another kind of "lawman").

In an open-ended social structure it is essential to spell out the practical limits of a freedom that is theoretically absolute and to regulate the conflicts that it brings about. This explains the incredibly complex and precise language of contracts (not to mention their enormous length), especially in the business world. Often enough it takes dozens of lawyers working together for weeks to settle the terms of a joint enterprise by two companies. If European corporations have long had a dismal track record in America, it is mostly because of their failure to realize that on the other side of the Atlantic a good lawyer is much more important than a chief engineer or a marketing specialist.

Even the work of the federal government consists primarily of legal matters. American political administrators, unlike their French counterparts, do not busy themselves with all the details of implementation. They issue neither decrees nor guidance letters. It falls to the judge to interpret the will of the legislator (who generally had tried to remain vague enough to keep everybody satisfied). This leads to interminable rounds of litigation and the hiring of formidable battalions of lawyers, who perform prodigious feats of procedural skill. The gigantic suit brought by the federal government against IBM for violation of antitrust laws will long remain a classic in this genre. Hundreds of lawyers had already worked for more than ten years on this case. A large building in Washington had to be rented by IBM simply for its lawyers' offices, and the whole affair has turned out to be so complicated that people increasingly wondered whether the government would be obstinate enough to see it through to the finish. Ronald Reagan's election finally brought an end to the antitrust case. The government dropped the suit.

In the realm of private life citizens have to keep a weather eye out to protect themselves even in the most trivial areas. Anything at all, in this litigious era, can land you in court. If you invite a friend to your swimming pool and he slips on the cement apron and breaks his leg, he may very well sue you for damages, claiming that your pool was badly maintained. A noted French journalist, Alain Clément, recently described the case of a man who was ordered to pay $80,000 in damages for having engaged with his best friend's wife in "culpable intercourse over the phone." This decision, by the way, was rendered *after* the wife had divorced her husband and married the defendant.[5]

In view of this extraordinary proliferation of lawsuits, the question comes to mind immediately: How can Americans, as open, trusting, and generous as they are, have gotten so obsessed with the law? Such barratry would seem much more appropriate among the French, who are born suspicious and, in keeping with the familiar stereotype, are forever worrying about how to defend themselves against the state, against society, against everybody. This is quite a paradox, and it touches the heart of the issue of individual freedom. Americans refuse the least interference with their theoretically free condition, and because of this they have stumbled into a legalistic quagmire. By contrast the French, who can tolerate the yoke of social and administrative limitations, spend their time building defenses against them but don't go to courts. They secure their freedom by withdrawing into themselves and living with limits. The Frenchman's motto might be, "My glass is a little one, but I drink out of my glass." American exuberance strikes him as megalomaniacal, just as the Frenchman's systematic mistrust strikes an American as mean spirited.

With his genius for existential perception, Solzhenitsyn is profoundly aware of this American "disease." In his address to the students at Harvard he may have shocked the American intelligentsia (carried away by his ardent anticommunism, he accused Americans of having let their courage fail them in Vietnam), but that in no way diminishes the remarkable relevance of his critical attack on what he denounced as a positive legal delirium.

". . . Every conflict is solved according to the letter of the law and this is considered to be the ultimate solution. If one is right from a legal point of view, nothing more is required, nobody may mention that one could still not be entirely right, and urge self-restraint or a renunciation of these rights, call for sacrifice and selfless risk: this would simply sound absurd. Voluntary self-restraint is almost unheard of: everybody strives toward further expansion to the extreme limit of the legal frames. . . .

"I have spent all my life under a communist regime and I will tell you that a society without any objective legal scale is a terrible one indeed. But a society with no other scale but the legal one is also less that worthy of man."[6]

This diatribe by the great Russian dissident, speaking to the West-

---

[5] Alain Clément, *Le Monde*, VII, 23, 1980.
[6] Alexander Solzhenitsyn, "A World Split Apart."

ern world, is particularly on target as regards the United States— undoubtedly the country where that passion for law has been pressed the farthest, to the edge of madness.

The Vicious Circle of Procedure

I have already mentioned in the first chapter how I fell in love with America at an early age, not least of all because I was struck by the sharp contrast between the freedom that has reigned there from the beginning and the stifling French bureaucracy to which I have devoted a large part of my research. French society is, at bottom, anarchic, and for this very reason it has developed a long hierarchical and bureaucratic tradition, designed to keep that libertarian behavior within the limits of civilized collective life. But this pattern of self-imposed restraints is the root cause of innumerable vicious circles. At the bottom of the scale people fend off abuse from the higher-ups by hiding the truth from them, as far as possible. This forces leaders to govern solely by means of abstract rules, always inadequate and hard to apply, which further incites the indignation of the governed, who refuse even more stubbornly to provide information, and so on.

This is a true source of innumerable jokes like the one about the future technocrat at the École Polytechnique learning how to solve several enormously difficult and fabulously complex equations in order to boil an egg. The system can function only because of the existence of parallel power structures, which are relentlessly pursued by the government and all its agencies, but which are forever cropping up. These subterranean networks, inspired by the universal need for action and influence, indicate just how much life there is in the body politic. And good leaders know how to make use of them, how to profit by what used to be called "le système D" (resourcefulness or wangling, from *se débrouiller*) by turning it toward broader social objectives.

It took me a long time to discover that America too had its vicious circles, no less stifling than the ones in France. I had seen, of course, those Rube Goldberg cartoons of absurdly complicated machines that serve in the end merely to sharpen a pencil, I had read fierce (but highly partisan) attacks on the federal administration and the rising tide of bureaucracy, but I did not really pay attention to them. It was the students I taught at Harvard who straightened me out on this point. Without their tireless efforts to educate me, I would probably never have come to doubt that the system was on the whole a good

106

thing. But they insisted on showing me that they were at least as "messed up" as we are,[7] and they are right.

To be convinced one need only take a slightly closer look at the American scene, applying the same analytical methods that one would in France. What throws the French observer off is that the vicious circles in America are different from the ones at home. Too preoccupied by their own failings, the French have a hard time seeing that instead of centralization and the abstract deductive reasoning that goes along with it these vicious circles grow out of juridical freedom and the accompanying passion for due process.

If you refuse to base the public order on a hierarchy, then you have to find some other way (and there really are no good ones) to regulate social intercourse. Constant recourse to court decisions, although it offers certain advantages, also has enormous drawbacks, in particular the vicious circles of the short term and of specialization.

I have already mentioned the bad effects of short-term thinking in the domain of politics, but the phenomenon is much more widespread. America is a society that lives in the whirlwind of the moment, because, with all conflicts being settled by litigation and all the risks from relationships with others being framed by law, the most pressing need is to be legally invulnerable. Now the law, and most of all perhaps American law, knows nothing of the future and cannot make any allowance for development, learning opportunities, or the complexity of human evolution.[8] All that matters is the immediate meaning of the facts under examination. To return to the preposterous example cited above, it makes no difference that once Mr. and Mrs. X have gotten divorced, the wrong done to Mr. X in the past from telephone conversations between his wife and the man she subsequently married seems quite minimal: the fact of those calls, and that fact alone, and only at the instant when they occurred, will be taken into consideration. Under such conditions it becomes essential for citizens to be on guard at every moment against every contingency. And all this goes on within a short-term context because nobody can plead good intentions. The problem is compounded for organizations, especially government bodies, which have to go to extraordinary lengths to put

[7]One of the positive achievements of the postwar period is the rivalry in self-criticism that has come over Western societies: each tries to prove that it has more shortcomings than the other. The Americans had been laggards in this round of denunciation, but Vietnam has enabled them to catch up.

[8]Hence American judicial practice rejects discussions of motivation—which French judges find so passionately interesting—and sticks to the facts. However admirable in some ways, this approach shuts off all reference to future development.

themselves out of range of their opponents. One could not invoke a higher interest, not even reasons of state.

This passion for staying above legal reproach is not without a certain grandeur. And French political writers are not necessarily wrong to cite it as a model for their own government, which sheds criticism like a raincoat in a shower, and which always thinks it knows best what everybody needs. But the American way of doing things can have some very negative consequences. What it amounts to is that once you are on the right side of the law, you can do anything. There is no supreme ombudsman, well informed by jealous observers, to worry about the (blameworthy?) reasons for your success. There will be no going back over the past. But make sure of the present, and be quick about it.

Thus the whirlwind of the short term: the more defensive moves anyone makes, the more others have to do the same, and so on. Suppose that a company is having some momentary problems, just when it is being watched by a conglomerate awaiting the right moment to move in. As soon as it does anything foolish, the conglomerate will make a killing on the stock market by snapping it up at a low price, thanks to an artfully managed takeover bid, and then selling it at a much higher one, after refloating it, more or less artificially. Such perfectly legal maneuvers can shield extraordinary swindles, and to prevent it the government has imposed draconian auditing rules. But audits simply increase the pressure on management from the short term. And if the job of financial operators has been made more difficult by prohibitions against the more glaring forms of cheating, the scope of their activity has been broadened by the establishment of across-the-board—but illusory—accountability.[9]

In the same way, the protection afforded workers by union contracts can have perverse effects. A company can fire a thousand people overnight if it loses a big customer. Provided it respects the terms agreed on in collective bargaining, which oblige it to follow the rule of seniority, nothing prevents it from adjusting its work force to fit the existing market. It makes temporary gains this way but at the cost of keeping on an underskilled, all-purpose corps of employees. The union's protective function, which guarantees that the employer will

[9]The complexity of the legal maneuvers involved in a major takeover bid and the tremendous efforts and costs incurred by all the parties involved have been documented in an extraordinary thorough and precise account of the day to day bargaining positions of all the actors in the Martin Marietta versus Bendix case by Hope Lampert, *Till Death Do Us Part* (Harcourt Brace Jovanovich, 1983).

not take any discriminatory action, pays little heed to their common future, only to short-term arrangements.

Consider the still thornier problems created by equal rights for minorities. The most striking feature about recent measures passed with this end in mind is their extreme haste. Americans waited for centuries to get upset over racism, but once they did become upset and it was decided to amend the laws, the cry went up for total and immediate equality. Often enough, of course, judges would grant delays in implementing the new legislation, but the delays were only technical. Nobody had thought out the difficulties that individuals would face in learning new social roles nor, a fortiori, the infinitely more complex issues that arise when a whole system of human relations is transformed, and when not just the individual but the collectivity has to go through a kind of social learning.

This has led not only to open resistance but also to all sorts of arrangements for thwarting the law. Since the Chinese and East Indians have managed to get themselves included in the same minority category as blacks, Ph.D.s from Hong Kong and Bombay may be invited to hold jobs for which qualified blacks cannot be found. Increasingly, people try to get around the law and, as a natural response, the law and the courts become more finicky. Here too the short term wins the day. The wider interests of the black minority, and its evolution over time, are completely ignored, provided the same magical percentage of privileged blacks can be attained in all public activities. In the meantime ghetto blacks are forgotten, as they sink deeper into the moral misery of drugs and welfare.

Another example: the struggle by the federal government against pollution. The results have been far below expectations, and certainly not in line with the enormous budget allotments. Yet this has not prevented the elaboration of a minutely detailed body of law, whose immense volume alone suffices to make it both incoherent and absurd.[10]

Americans, to be sure, do not stop short at protecting themselves; they also know how to wheel and deal. True, collusion, if not always prohibited, is subject to strict surveillance. Some important business leaders (a president of General Electric, for example) have been given

[10]For the last years of the Carter presidency, an attempt was made to simplify regulation and to deregulate. The Reagan presidency moved much more brutally, but seems to have found the job to be harder than it had imagined. Environment is certainly less well protected but the complexity of the legal procedures have not been especially reduced.

prison sentences for illegal restraint of trade. But who could believe for a moment that there is less fraud in America than in Europe? The rigidity of the system bans commonsense arrangements as illegal, thereby fueling America's underground economy, which could not prosper as it does unless it had an indispensable social function. And here too the country slips into a vicious circle: the more reality gets out of hand, the more people try to control it with the only means they know, that is, the legal regulation that caused the problem to begin with.

Another kind of vicious circle, closely connected with the short-term pressure grows out of specialization. The spirit of the American legal system, in order to assure the individual his right to total freedom, tends to define his functions, rights, and duties in the most precise detail. The boundaries of the individual's territory are marked off; once that has been done he need not take orders from anyone. According to the logic of the system, by pursuing his own personal interests within this carefully defined framework, he will contribute to the common good without even trying to. The French, Americans say, are forever meddling in everyone else's business, whence the messy confusion intrinsic to their system. In contrast Americans know how to show personal initiative while staying in their place, which makes for better order and more efficiency.

Within certain limits this analysis is correct. As long as the problems to be handled are not too complex, the American approach is faster and more effective. But specialization carried to extremes can also, and very quickly, give rise to aberrations. Confident of his rights, any given employee may develop his own set of principles and build up his own clientele, ignoring the consequences this might have for the broader interests of the organization he belongs to or the public at large. Government administration, particularly in the areas of health and education, has become increasingly paralyzed by this phenomenon, and business has also been affected.

It is against this sort of bureaucracy that Ivan Illich has raised the banner of revolt. Romantic as his attacks may seem, they point up an absolutely crucial problem, which the procedural model for settling conflicts, as opposed to the European or Japanese hierarchical model, makes considerably worse. Contrary to its popular image, America has little talent for cooperation and concerted action. The Japanese method, which depends upon a symbiosis between the government bureaucracy and the business world, is totally foreign, even incomprehensible to Americans. So is the French method: the French spend their time coordinating their moves with one another, panic-stricken by the thought of overlapping assignments—which sometimes causes an official to do nothing at all, so as not to risk encroaching upon a neighbor, who is likewise doing nothing at all. This would be unthinkable in the United States, but Americans suffer from another form of anarchy: their feudal power bases, endlessly quarreling with one another, are nonetheless practically untouchable. Each one, firmly entrenched behind its rights, reconstructs the rest of society in its own image and likeness. Only the federal administration (and, within that, the only comprehensive executive office, the presidency) can really ensure coordination. But, owing to the very growth implied by this unique power, the federal administration has become a hopelessly tangled jungle.

One of the favorite forms of activity of the United States federal system is regulation: Congress eventually, at the request of the president, continually provides new rules which the federal regulatory commissions will have the duty to make the public observe. These commissions impose strict regulations on their field of surveillance, but, as often happens, the remedy fast becomes worse than the disease. The implementation of each measure passed stirs up gigantic legal battles, with armies of lawyers making their living from the business of regulation. How different it all is from France, where, though everyone agrees there is far too much legislation, people pay so little attention to it that laws sink into oblivion. (I know of one case where the government pushed through a law that was already on the books.) In general, the pressing need for social regulation felt by all modern societies has brought down on the United States a rash of totally misconceived but legally binding rules. The last few years especially have seen an unbelievable proliferation of them. The United States is suffering from a rage for juridical procedure that is undoubtedly much more disturbing than the regulatory mania that certain French administrations have been justly accused of fostering.[11] The text of rules sent to the prefectural administrations by the French Ministry of Public Works averages 1,100 pages per month. But the American Environmental Protection Agency alone was sending out 50 percent more in 1980. This swollen mass of paper is matched by a comparable growth in the number of civil servants. Up to 1980 France had managed to stop the spread of bureaucracy: secretaries have stopped knitting on the job. But a few years ago in one section of an American

[11]The *Los Angeles Times* series, mentioned previously, give many details of this mania.

111

government agency with several hundred employees, work came to a halt for three weeks because the budget allotment for typewriter ribbons was exhausted.

Legal Madness and Government by Judges

To understand the excesses that America's juridical obsession can lead to, one might reflect on two critically important issues: public assistance and racial and sexual equality.

There is no more painful problem, both morally and socially, in America today than public assistance, usually designated by the imprecise and ironically ill-chosen term, welfare. Official, legally mandated assistance has now replaced the old, humiliating traditional charity. Having become a right, it no longer insults the recipient's human dignity. But it has perverse results, which grow more and more disastrous as the amount of aid increases. It has to be recalled that private charity, despite everything, was not without its advantages: its paternalism went hand in hand with a certain human warmth. Insufficient by itself, it nonetheless took the whole person, or the whole family, into consideration. Finally, it allowed for some flexibility by adapting to changing situations. Public assistance, however, establishes a right—or rather, a series of extremely complicated rights— that sooner or later transforms the people who have those rights into litigants, to be taken care of by specialized lawyers. Welfare rights are managed by separate and independent bureaucracies, in accordance with the rule of specialization, so that the families under their jurisdiction are harassed by a small host of caseworkers and supervisors. Help is never given in a single package, nor does it take into account the possibilities for transformation in the recipient's situation.

It all has vicious consequences. The best known, and one that has been the subject of innumerable debates, is the disruption of the black family, owing to the fact that special allocations are given to families without a father. The text of the law makes no sexist distinctions and deals in principle with single-parent families. But in a society that remains sexist, the problem really concerns the absence or disappearance of the father. Families living in economic misery were very quick to grasp their obvious financial interest in getting the father written off as having deserted the household—whence the classic subterfuge of the father who vanishes when the social worker comes to call.

What this law does in effect is pay a high premium to couples living together outside of marriage and reinforces the matriarchal culture of the underclass, especially in the black ghettos. One of the outcomes is that black children grow up fatherless and masculine roles become devalued or pushed in irresponsible directions. A law made to protect the dignity of the person contributes in reality to degrade the character of a whole social group. It is clear that even if nobody dares to speak frankly about this deplorable situation (neither among blacks nor the vast liberal majority of the American population), the connection between public assistance, the disintegration of the black family, and the subculture based on drugs and petty theft is a very strong one in the collective consciousness of America. A particularly reactionary congressman from Texas once proposed that women signing up for welfare be obliged to get sterilized after their third child: he could not see why American taxpayers should have to foot the bill for future muggers. The idea provoked widespread outrage, but it *was* discussed.

Many specialists have been working time and again to get to the roots of this dramatic problem. The Nixon administration tried hard to institute a negative income tax. Debate over the whole issue, unfortunately, went nowhere because the key participants in it were jurists, and their arguments were based on decisions made by judges.

American jurists display a serious inability to recognize the existence of social groups as such and to understand the ultimate consequences that laws can have for those groups. They limit themselves to the question of whether it is fair that so-and-so receives this or that amount of aid and under what conditions. When Daniel Patrick Moynihan tried to discuss the problems that welfare poses for black families, he ran into spirited protests not just from black leaders but from the bulk of the liberal community. He had dared to point up the existence of a social reality beyond the matter of individual rights.

The jurists are opposed, of course, by the economists, guardians of financial rationality, and partisans of schemes like the negative income tax. But economic reasoning proves to be utterly powerless against the logic of rights, as supported by the legal professions and the bureaucracies that make their living from that system. Furthermore, the bureaucrats seem to have the weight of human reality on their side, since the economists have not been able to come up with anything but abstract (if appealing) formulas.

Thus, despite appearances, America is ruled not by the new rationality of cost/benefit analysis but by the traditional rationality of jurists. One might say, to stretch things a bit, that the government is in the hands not of the politicians nor of the businessmen but of the judges: that is, of those who "declare the law" (cf. the Latin *jurisdictio*).

Otherwise the country governs itself. The importance of this government by judges, is particularly evident, apart from the welfare system,
in the area of racial and sexual discrimination, which for the past
twenty years has been the hottest issue on the American scene. The
most debated problems, school busing, the quota system, and affirmative action are first of all legal affairs that have become the preserve
of the judges and of the legal profession. Judges will organize in great
detail the conditions, extent, and timing of a busing system. Judges
could step in and verify whether any organization, public or private,
has done its best to assure an equitable mix of races and sexes.

What is the logic behind the twenty-five-year period that opened
with a momentous Supreme Court decision in 1954? It is a legal logic
and not a political one. In *Brown* vs. *The Board of Education of Topeka*
the justices overturned a long precedent sanctioning the right of local
authorities to maintain "separate but equal" schools for blacks and
whites, because these schools did not guarantee black citizens their
equal rights under the Constitution. This memorable decision gave
the signal for a long series of efforts to desegregate the schools. Lawsuits were filed everywhere, and gradually judges got around to en-
forcing the new ruling and ordered local authorities to move in one
way or another toward integration.

The Court acted on its own in this matter, taking the place of
Congress, which was too hamstrung by Southerners to do anything.
Not until 1964, after the assassination of President Kennedy, was the
civil rights bill passed which the court had paved the way for. But this
law would have been gutted by amendments (if it had passed at all),
had it not been for the combination of the moral crisis brought on
by the assassination and the clever maneuvering of President Johnson,
who was determined to push through the work of his predecessor.
And, as we have seen, it was only because of the confusion reigning
in Congress then that a rider was approved, almost inadvertently,
which ended up having some important consequences: the paragraph
concerning discrimination against women. After the law passed, the
president was able to set up the Office of Economic Opportunity,
charged with overseeing its implementation in both the public and
private sector and with prosecuting delinquents. In 1965 the OEO
was authorized to apply the principle of Affirmative Action, which
reversed the burden of proof: the plaintiff no longer needed to prove
that he had been discriminated against; instead, the company or government bureau was called upon to show that it had gone to sufficient
lengths to end all discrimination among its personnel.

The logic of all this is clear enough: faced with a Congress incapable of reaching a decision and with an executive branch with the best of intentions but too weak to impose its will, the justices, drawing on the Constitution and existing precedents, dictated to a vacillating and divided country the way it had to behave. With the whole legal system behind them, they gave orders and made sure they were carried out. An immense mechanism responded to their moral directives and swung into action: the legislative and executive branches followed the judiciary. Liberals hailed the justices and the courage displayed by the courts, which alone managed to keep the American dream alive. In one sense it could be said that during this period the problem of civil rights dominated the internal life of American society even more than the problem of union rights from the thirties to the fifties. The labor movement had already leaned heavily on the law, but this time the courts took matters directly into their own hands.[12] And, across a much broader front, they invaded all sorts of other domains, such as consumer rights or environmental pollution. Their jurisdiction now extends to the quality of life.

What has resulted from this growth in judicial authority? First of all, a remarkable social transformation. It is beyond dispute that in a few years blacks have made more progress than in the whole century following the Civil War. Whatever the costs and the secondary consequences, the overall effect has been mostly positive. The United States has gotten rid of a problem that had it morally paralyzed and that was a stumbling block to all its efforts at reform and social development. Without a doubt the very bluntness of the Supreme Court's decree was necessary to break the iron circle where both an oppressed minority and a guilty, impotent majority thrashed about. Nonetheless, if this decision seems in retrospect to be the most positive act of internal policy since the days of the New Deal, one cannot help worrying about the disproportionate part in the nation's life which has now been conferred upon judges, as well as about the now familiar sight of their governing by injunction, ordinance, and decree. In fact, it is no longer just the traditional reactionaries and small-town bigots who are distressed over the future of American institutions: they have been joined by neoconservative—and sometimes liberal—intellectuals.

To grasp the full extent of the problem, one first has to know who the judges are. The majority of them are elected, but they are not the ones who count: the nine justices of the Supreme Court and the six hundred or so federal appellate judges—all nominated by the

---

[12]Judges played a large role in the liberalism of the thirties, forties, and fifties. It was a judicial institution, the National Labor Relations Board, that made possible the development of the new strain of American unionism (the CIO).

president and, once appointed, permanent fixtures. Highly esteemed,[13] well paid, quite competent, well organized and efficient, they are also, apart from their specific function, genuine political personages—who, unlike other politicians, enjoy the incalculable advantage of stability. In the Supreme Court there is not even a fixed retirement age, so that the political and ideological bent of the Court is determined entirely by the wishes of the various presidents who happen to be in office when justices die or retire.[14] For a long time the Court remained a conservative institution, whose essential role seemed to be to protect traditions and principles from any revolutionary notions that might occur to impulsive presidents. Thus in 1933 it was the Supreme Court that blocked the first—and largely corporatist—reforms proposed by Franklin Delano Roosevelt. It was not until the end of the fifties that the Supreme Court, spurred on by Chief Justice Earl Warren, a former governor of California and liberal Republican appointed by Eisenhower, turned from surveillance to active reform.

Critics ask nowadays: Why should judges bear a larger share of the responsibility for the common good than do elected representatives of the people? Is it the democratic thing to let the judge's bench replace the ballot box? Historically, judges were supposed to be wise and experienced guardians of tradition, upholding it against intemperate assaults by the president, Congress, or state legislatures. But this function cannot be pressed too far without danger, and when it expands into the area of reform, there are reasons to fear that democracy may be left behind altogether. One wonders what right judges have to become involved in every social issue, and why they should be making the decisions, instead of politicians, who in principle have the actual responsibility.

For myself, I would argue from another angle. As I see it, the great danger implicit in government by judges is not so much that it will stray from the path of democracy or upset the remarkable constitutional equilibrium that Americans have always known in the past but rather that it accentuates a deep—and unfortunate—trend already present in American society: the rage for procedure, which is particularly dysfunctional in a world as complex as ours. Government by judges is the most significant symptom of "the trouble with Amer-

[13]This is absolutely not the case with the rest of the legal profession, whose prestige has plummeted.

[14]For many liberals the only really serious argument against Ronald Reagan's candidacy was that, given the age and health of several of the justices, he will get to choose a number of appointees to the Court.

ica." A society that is no longer capable of getting hold of itself, and so afraid of making choices that it shifts the burden to the judiciary, that society must inevitably suffer a kind of hardening of the arteries, even if in the short run this or that decision by the court may be tremendously progressive.

"You don't change society by decrees"—if I may quote the title of my last book—whether in America or France.[15] You cannot command the world to transform itself in accord with your wishes just because you think you have found the magic formula for justice or the common good. That kind of presumption leads to two disastrous consequences, the first of which is fairly obvious and one that I have already dealt with—the creation of a restricted caste with a monopoly over the decision-making process—but nobody seems to have noticed the second: a profound transformation in the very nature of public debate. In America today that debate has been shifted entirely to the courts. The quality of life as well as personal happiness (why not? after all, the right of every individual to seek it is written into the Declaration of Independence) become simple legal issues capable of being resolved by fair-minded, distributive measures. The entire social system increasingly comes to revolve around this static juridical debate, which misses the essential point, namely, change and development.

One may ask how American society, which has always been considered a model of dynamism and practicality, can now be going through this paradoxical reversal. It is hard to believe that the country can surrender so unconditionally to jurists and accountants who lay down the law with no regard for common sense and no feeling for reality. The fact is, no doubt, that American tradition is not as simple as had been believed, and that the pursuit of happiness, while a dynamic factor in a time of conquest, can help to bring on social sclerosis in a time of saturation.

---

[15]Michel Crozier, *On ne change pas la societé par decret* (Paris: Fayard, 1979), translated into English under the title *Strategies for Change* (Cambridge, Mass.: MIT Press, 1982).

CHAPTER SEVEN

DEMON VIRTUE

FOR A LONG TIME, IT WAS fashionable in France to talk about the "French disease," the price Frenchmen have to pay for their deep, visceral attachment to centralized bureaucracy.[1] By the same standards one could talk now of the "American disease," the curse Americans cannot get rid of because of their fanatical commitment to the formalism of due process.

This way of speaking may be useful as a shock to awaken people from their complacency. There is no such thing, however, as an "American disease" or for that matter a "French disease." Any culture is at once everything and its opposite, not so much because societies are crazy quilts, haphazardly assembled out of groups with different traditions, but because people are by nature contradictory and cannot live together in strict obedience to a single principle or a single set of principles, relatively coherent and hierarchically arranged. The French, who reputedly have a stay-at-home temperament, have always been notable explorers, adventurers, and missionaries. Madly in love with centralization, they are also ungovernable anarchists.

---

[1] See Alain Peyrefitte, *The Trouble with France* (New York: Alfred Knopf, 1981), published in Paris as *Le mal français* (Paris: Plan, 1976).

In the same way Americans are at the same time self-assured entrepreneurs and finicky, mistrustful legalists, both champions of permissiveness and true believers trembling before a wrathful Calvinist God. In any one culture there will always be several ways to solve or evade any given problem, and this diversity shows every sign of being not just functional but strictly indispensable. Listing the contradictory features present in one society after another never lacks a certain piquant effect, but the underlying point is knowing what those characteristics indicate. One might argue, with some overstatement, that culture is a composite of all the troubles which people make for one another so they can manage to live together and of the ways they resolve them. The genius of Tocqueville was to realize, before anyone else, the problematic and instrumental character of culture—with all its consequences.

The overall configuration, however, has a definite pattern, and this pattern shows a high degree of permanence. It is an answer to the problems societies face, but at the same time it imposes its well-rounded solutions to any kind of problem, up to a point, however, because there are limits and natural constraints. This human construct has to adapt, and usually it can adapt. Despite a powerful tendency to stay as it is and a capacity for savage resistance to novelty, it often succeeds in adapting quickly and well. People are capable of finding new solutions, generally within the framework of accepted principles, but sometimes through the introduction of new principles. In the course of this evolutionary process one meets with happy moments and moments of degradation, with spirals of development and regression. As long as it remains within certain confines, a system will function well and develop normally. But once a given threshold is passed, the spiral of development is reversed, and one enters a regressive spiral. When we are unable to understand those thresholds properly, every downturn strikes us as a tragic surprise. Then, just as unexpectedly, we see the system transform itself and make a fresh start: evil has been metamorphosed into good.

In this sense, but in this sense only, it is worthwhile to speak of the American disease as what is wrong with America—or France or England for that matter. That kind of focusing can be especially useful now as regards America, since over the last thirty years American society has been too often employed as a touchstone for other societies. If they were looking to the American model of efficiency, they were on the right track. Anything that slowed up adaptation to that model was bad. The recent emergence of this American disease, no less virulent than those affecting other societies, has finally made us see

119

the relative nature of our vision and acknowledge that there is no one universal perfect model.

Simplistic Faith in Human Goodness

Ever since the eighteenth century Western thinkers have been proclaiming that man is born good and that society is perfectible. But in their heart of hearts they do not quite believe it. Reality is there to remind us that evil persists and worst of all that pursuing the good with too much enthusiasm may often bring deplorable results. The road to hell, as they say, is paved with good intentions.

Every society has its own way of resolving its problems with good and evil through choices that are metaphysical and, in the final analysis, religious. Still, the solution it comes up with constitutes a general principle of social organization which belongs to a realm beyond the feelings and opinions of individuals and beyond any abstract arguments. The American solution is unquestionably the most radical of all, at least in the West. The Americans have quite simply decided not to believe in evil.[2] Their ideal world could be described as an eighteenth-century pastoral scene, where everyone wears a modest little wig—no extravagant papists here—making sure to appear neat, properly powdered, smiling, the perfect social creature.[3] I want to stress the social character of this ideal. Metaphysics can be fitted into it, if you insist, but on condition that everyone keeps his own system to himself and that it remain a pastoral metaphysics, powdered and well behaved, as in Ingmar Bergman's film of *The Magic Flute*.[4] The point at issue, then, is not the meaning of human destiny but the rules of the game.

To understand the American system, one has to realize that its faith in goodness is widespread and absolute but not very deep. For the individual, it is a sort of Pascalian bet: stupefy yourself, it is more efficient. And for society it is a kind of sweeping assumption that

[2]If we are to believe Aleksandr Zinoviev, only the Soviets have found an equally radical solution: they do not believe in good. See Aleksandr Zinoviev, *The Radiant Future* (New York: Random House, 1980) and *The Yawning Heights* (New York: Random House, 1980).

[3]The reader may object that Puritanism, like Jansenism, was elitist and hence believed in evil. The just were few in number, and ideal goodness could be achieved only by those who were touched by grace. But this combative posture, upholding the rigor of the law against the laxity of the old structures, underwent a transformation beginning in the first half of the seventeenth century. Goodness was now within everyone's reach, and the descendants of the sons of the austere pilgrims became proselytes for equality. By making grace available to one and all, they in effect denied evil.

[4]The Swedes too believe in goodness.

recalls Rousseau's social contract: if everyone decides to believe in the goodness of man, we shall be able to trust one another, and everything will run more efficiently in this society whose dynamics have been so profoundly based on trust. This assumption has, in fact, shown itself to be extraordinarily efficient. Even if reality does not resemble this fictional version except in a limited way, the individual's "wager" will in general pay off. And on the social level over the past three hundred years the development of this new culture has proved the fruitfulness of the assumption. The commonly shared feeling of trust permits a much larger and faster mobilization of resources, leading to a vast number of spiraling patterns, whether of civic virtue or economic development. It becomes possible to interact more efficiently and, above all, more rapidly with more people, one can try out more solutions with more freedom. And you eat your lunch faster.

Seen from Europe in 1950, the society of trust looked like the very image of progress, modern management, and unlimited expansion. Europeans were inspired by it, and they had good reason to be: the system worked for them too. But they did not fully implement it, because of social resistance to it and because of their deep-rooted skepticism. And now, thirty years later, we see that nowhere is the model working so badly as in the United States itself: the dynamics of trust increasingly promote failure and discourage innovation. The truth is that living by the assumption of trust in no way means the same as living in trust. And when the gap between theory and reality grows too wide, the wager is no longer winnable and the assumption becomes, in American parlance, counterproductive. Yet why should this gap be wider now than before? Simply because the postwar world has become infinitely more complicated than the innocent (both within and without its borders) universe that America had lived in until then. In this situation the model of a society based on trust proves much too simplistic: it is, when all is said and done, a binary system (yes/ no: trust/mistrust) that prevents people from forming complex human relations as well as understanding—with a view to adjusting—the manifold interlocking strategies deployed by human feelings, with their infinite nuances.

Let us try to grasp the consequences of postulating trust in a tremendously complex world. At first blush it seems to offer an immense advantage: one can communicate better, more quickly, with more people, hence one ought to be able to cooperate more easily, and to do an increasingly better job of resolving increasingly complicated problems. But then why do the Japanese, who communicate slowly and obliquely, hobbled by their codes of politeness and their

121

love of circumlocution, succeed so well in adapting to this complex world—so much better than the Americans? For that matter, why do the French, forever suspicious and sniffing out hidden motives and backroom maneuvers, manage to muddle through fairly well?

As I see it, the only way to explain it is to move beyond the notion of efficiency operating through simplification: thanks to their postulate, Americans are capable of solving the simplest problems, with tremendous rapidity, but the importance of those problems is constantly decreasing. From now on preference has to be given to a logic of complexity. Look at the question in a different way: when you live by the assumption that goodness is supreme, you are obliged to suppress evil, to deny its existence. "No one is intentionally wicked," thought Plato; bad people were all unfortunates. So you buy all the perfumes of Araby to wipe away the little spot of blood and, since you are only human, you put on a hypocritical mask. But hypocrisy helps evil prosper and, though suppressed, from time to time it comes back. Then you have a scandal, and there is no way to restore the status quo except by recourse to the God of wrath.

These "binary" mechanisms give American culture a very hard, sharp-edged look. Evil is somewhere else, it is the very essence of our enemies. One passes from light to darkness with no twilight zone. Thus, superficially at least, the United States is paradise, I never met a man I didn't like, and so on. But behind this optimistic front all sorts of dishonest practices flourish and spread. The more the realm of light is taken to be flawless, the more the realm of darkness grows. When the frontier was still open, the process of national expansion made it possible to whitewash the evil done: the cheating and stealing of the early days were redeemed by later good conduct—once success was safely in hand. But when the system reaches its limits and is closed off, one inevitably returns to the God of wrath and looks for scapegoats. Then that God strikes, and without mercy, and one has to hunt up all the shady arrangements and little compromises for which Latin tradition, with its tolerant old sinners' viewpoint, always finds attenuating circumstances.

This American lack of charity, of indulgence, of "mercy" in the medieval sense, is not just a moral problem; it also has some immediate practical consequences. Rapid, effective communication in ordinary situations is of no use when difficulties arise that challenge binary logic and leave its users utterly baffled. This logic, with its absolutes of good and evil—"Did he violate the law? Answer yes or no."—becomes, when the answer is negative, not simply inhuman but stupid, the blind, bureaucratic "I-don't-want-to-know-about-it." It is the logic

that explains the American passion for litigation, the rage for due process. All this brings on an extraordinary incapacity for understanding the other person, for meeting him in depth, for putting oneself in his place, for reasoning in terms of complex strategy. The level of efficiency suddenly drops once the problem calls for more than simple binary logic.

By no means should we conclude that American society knows nothing of tolerance—which reigns supreme in the Latin countries. Clearly, in many ways the reverse is true. But tolerance and intolerance do not mean the same things in America and, say, France, which explains a number of habitual misunderstandings. For example, French society is tolerant out of skepticism. Whatever else of Christianity it may have rejected, it still likes to ask, "Who are you to be throwing the first stone at me?" Since we are all sinners to some extent, you must never go too far in condemning anyone.[5] American society will have nothing to do with such weakness, which it views, reasonably enough, as leading to conservatism. It has much more tolerance than French society for all sorts of opinions, beliefs, and eccentricities, as long as they remain compatible with the postulate of trust. Whatever cannot be fitted into that postulate, whatever, in other words, Americans cannot tolerate, is precisely what the French tolerate best.

This peculiarly American passion (one that owes much to their "enlightened" European ancestors) for man's intrinsic goodness, for freedom guaranteed by contract, for the right to the pursuit of happiness, ought to be considered, however simplistically it may manifest itself, as a grand achievement of the human spirit. It fueled the astonishing success of the American frontier—no more efficient model was ever employed to people a new land and found a new nation. Moreover, the American dream is also, to some degree, the European dream. Without it Europeans could have accomplished neither the sweeping economic development of the nineteenth century nor the spectacular reconstruction (with American help) after World War II. But at the same time this dream is terribly dangerous and threatens to pave the way to a cold, solitary world. "No man is an island"—John Donne's sermon sounded as a warning. In its archetypal form, the American West romance comes down to a husband, his wife, and a rifle—nothing else. From another angle, the American creed echoes the anarchist utopian cry: Neither God, nor Master. The Puritan's

[5]In this context the reader might think of the difference between the character of the French detective, the old trooper with all his experience and knowledge of people, and the American detective, the bloodhound eager to track down the guilty and confound them with his pitiless, airtight case.

God is so harsh that he had to be rejected in the abstract. And in regard to poorer relations, Americans pretend they do not really exist. As a rule they reject the idea of man's power over his fellows—which prevents them from grasping the complexities of power and the difficulties involved in any advanced social learning. In their eyes everyone ought to know what he wants right from the first, and ought to be able to get it, if he abides by the contract.

The French, their heads always full of casuistic odds and ends, are better prepared than Americans to think holistically, to look at a complete system, with its peculiar complexities. Of course, the French also have a powerful Jansenist tradition, and there are more than a few Antigones in the country. But this duality, while it sometimes weakens the French, is also a strong cultural asset. Absurd as it may seem, Americans might be well advised to spend a little time studying seventeenth-century Jesuit moral theology, to look over their marvelously inventive casuistry,[6] so foreign to the mode of reasoning of the Puritan whose paradigm is the contract. For the casuist good and evil exist, naturally, but they always have to be viewed in context: what appeared at first to be black, from a legal standpoint, may turn gray when one allows for the situation and motives of the guilty party. And every condemnation of an individual must be measured against the social consequences it will have.

In any case, regardless of the Jesuits, Americans urgently need to realize that the era of the frontier is over, and that it is now their turn to enter the "time of saturation,"[7] into a world where, to be sure, they can hold onto their values only provided they learn to accept the existence of other values that can enrich them. Only then will it be possible for modes of reasoning better adapted to new conditions to emerge on the American scene.

The Dream of Permissive Education

There is no more deep-seated social problem than education, because it is through education that a society forms itself, knows itself, and achieves its identity. Education is at once the source and the expression of values. Hence the crisis in education is not just a problem but also signals a state of profound confusion. This crisis has been felt in all civilized countries, but much more severely in the United States than

[6]The thought of Spanish, and even the French, Jesuits of the early seventeenth century is much more subtle and sophisticated than is generally believed, with all due respect to Pascal.

[7]To use Pierre Chaunu's formulation of it.

elsewhere. In addition, the crisis in these other countries has broken out in connection with the typically American model of permissive education: the success of permissiveness, by nurturing boundless aspirations in so many individuals, has put the schools in a very difficult situation. They no longer have a clear idea of what they are doing, and citizens no longer know what they want from them. But when children cannot assimilate society's fundamental values, then their parents cannot recognize themselves in their offspring, cultural transmission becomes more and more difficult, and the very existence of society is threatened.

My friend Jim March, one of those rare academic personalities who is widely known and admired outside of academe, likes to argue the following paradox: "For a long time we have had two theories on the behavior of human beings. The first one applies to adults (they know what they want) and has been the basis of our understanding of economics and politics; the second refers to children (they are incapable of knowing what they really want), and we had used it to build our pedagogy. People have tried to unify the two theories, but they have taken the wrong approach: instead of admitting that adults themselves usually do not quite know what they want—and so are badly in need of learning—Americans now claim that children, just like adults, know what they want." This paradox is not as reactionary as it might first seem.

Fortunately for Europeans, the crisis they are going through is less intense than in America, because institutions, public officials at every level and, up to a certain point, the whole of society still retain some belief in the reality of evil. In France, for example, the leftists in the educational system, although they naturally believe in man's intrinsic goodness, continue to act as if they believed in original sin, passing on to their pupils this rather awkward message, if I may spoof it a bit: "In principle, you are good and society is bad. But in fact you know nothing, and hence you are only potentially good. Therefore, line up four by four, and I don't want to hear a pin drop."

However things may be in Europe, the crisis of American schooling is being played out, basically, on three levels: admissions standards, institutional functioning, and pedagogy. Despite its extreme simplicity, the problem of admissions is very serious and, in a way, insoluble. French schools used to be based on the principles of classification, differentiation, and, in a word, rejection. Even today, though it operates in an infinitely more subtle fashion, the French school remains a rejecting machine. Insofar as its ultimate purpose is to set up an objective and universally recognized hierarchy of individuals, this system of rejection seems relatively functional. But American schools, quite to the contrary, are founded on the idea of admitting everyone. Since it is thought of as being for one and all, the American school aims at giving each pupil equal attention and at keeping classification to a minimum. Of course, it has always "tracked" students, and much more than Americans were ever aware of. Children from privileged backgrounds went to good schools, became good students, and got into college. This situation tended to create a positive spiral: when teachers have good students, they are happy and proud, they do an increasingly better job of teaching their increasingly bright students. In this context permissiveness works, since everyone involved is full of goodwill. But once you try to end this hidden selectivity and to achieve genuinely equal opportunity, you break up the positive pattern, and permissiveness becomes dysfunctional, because good results depend upon high-quality students. Thus permissive democracy will not function well unless, paradoxically, it builds upon a preselected group. When it has to deal with an undifferentiated mass, the effect is purely and simply destructive.

To shed some more light on this paradox, let me offer an example from the medical profession. It is clear that if you measure medical efficiency by the rate of cure, in order to do good medicine, you need to have "good patients" who are susceptible to being cured. Our research group in France has studied an ideal case in point, that of kidney transplants. We compared four hospital wards. In the first two dialysis services, everything is going extremely well. Relations between doctors, nurses, and patients are splendid. Patients have high expectations of the transplant, their morale is excellent, and the rate of success is remarkable. This smooth performance is the result of an enormous effort on the part of the doctors and nurses to practice a more humane kind of medicine. But to do that they have had to choose their patients carefully, taking only moderate risks. Hence, since their patients have a good chance of recovering, it is possible to talk to them in a reasonable way about their disease and the danger of death. Then, when a death does occur, the whole community, both patients and medical staff, attends the funeral.

In the two other services studied, which unlike the first two accept anybody and everybody, the death rate is very high. Psychosomatic troubles are rampant, and patients view the prospect of the transplant with terror. Nobody talks to anyone else, personal relationships are difficult. It is not hard to analyze this painful contrast: the "mass effect" has transformed a positive pattern into a vicious circle, so that the final results are much worse than they should be. Put in this environment, even the "good" patients find their statistical chances of recovery much reduced.

Similarly, the American ideal of permissiveness has failed in the matter of school admissions. Not that the problem is theoretically insoluble. But the wholesale and immediate expansion of the best system available has led to the worst aberrations. On the one hand, the old selective arrangements go right back into operation: the good students, mostly from privileged environments, take flight to private schools. On the other, the public school system, weakened by these defections, is less capable than ever before of handling a heterogeneous mass of students, among whom any notions of responsibility quickly disintegrate. The lack of responsibility leads to a general regression, culminating in disorder and violence. The pastoral scene has become a jungle.

The problem of schools as institutions derives from the admissions problem, but it has nonetheless a certain independent status. Americans have been brought to the point of rediscovering the importance of institutions: schools will cease to function properly, if they become mere bureaucracies. To treat teachers as pawns and groups of students as interchangeable is to break the essential tool of all education. If you want to succeed in the immense task of assuring an education for everyone and to leaven it with enough permissiveness, you must have very good schools to begin with. Instead of being suspicious of the elite schools, under the pretext that they are creating castes and, by their selectiveness, promoting inequality, one should try to use them to promote excellence. There is only one way to proceed here: one has to accept reality, which is to say the existence of broad gaps in equality, in order to work toward filling them in. To deny them or try to suppress them overnight which is not that different is to court certain failure.

The upshot of it all is that permissiveness, as a working pedagogical assumption, has to be challenged. The social drift linked to the idea of permissiveness has made it counterproductive. For a pedagogy to be effective, it is certainly necessary for the learner to be active. But being active does not mean not making any effort. On the contrary, learning means changing oneself. It is not like buying a product in the supermarket: learning requires the one being taught to enter into a complex, often difficult, relationship with a teacher who necessarily has to jolt him, since he is forcing him to become something that he cannot know that he wishes to become. I trust the reader will understand that I am by no means recommending a return to the authoritarian education of years past, but if one wants children

127

to learn to make real choices, one first has to make them experiment, and give them the chance to outdo themselves. Permissiveness American-style comes down to a monotonous conjugation: I like you very much, you like me very much, we like each other very much. . . . The underlying idea (not a completely false one, by the way) is that students whose teachers think well of them work better than those whom they think badly of; it could be quite all right but for the obvious conclusion most people will jump on: think well of everyone, or, more bluntly, don't think at all, give up.

The most pressing need of schools in America, like those anywhere else, is for adults. No learning is possible without adults who can take responsibility for the child's development, can offer him a model while resisting his impulses, and can make decisions at the risk of making mistakes.

The Market and Virtue

Associating the market and virtue may shock some readers, but I use the phrase on purpose, because for Americans the market actually has an inherent virtue. And the market, which they regard with a genuine religious awe, also corresponds closely to the dream of permissiveness: it is the ideal place where everyone can meet on equal terms, in total freedom, with everything clear and aboveboard. Before attacking this notion, I would like to defend it. Europeans, especially Marxist Europeans, tend to cry out instantly: That's a fine freedom! It allows the people who have no means of protection to be more thoroughly exploited. This well-worn critique betrays a large blind spot: we must not forget where we are coming from and where we risk winding up.

At the beginning of the nineteenth century in Europe freedom of movement for the labor force was (and would still be in communist countries today) an eminently progressive measure. It meant, and means, the abolition of work permits, of all the vexations and red tape that prevented workers from leaving their boss. Furthermore, the labor market very often works in favor of the underdog. For many categories of workers it works very well. In any case when it is functioning reasonably well the market will sweep away many oppressive restrictions from the old days and prevent the emergence of new ones. Similarly, it is quite true that when the postulate of trust is concretely realized and when everybody plays fair and square—as occasionally happens—you get the best results imaginable. Finally, it must be repeated that even apart from such happy moments the market is in any event preferable to a monopolistic system, to collective farms, rationing, arbitrary quotas, long lines of customers outside stores, the black market, bribery, graft, and the rest.

To get down to the negative side, it is equally true that this idyllic, abstract vision of the market is actually an umbrella covering a very large number of different markets, organized in various ways, interdependent but largely autonomous. And many of these local or specialized markets, owing to their internal structure or their connections with other markets or their peculiar patterns of exchange, permit sundry kinds of cheating and fraud, provide a sanction for scandalous inequities, or prove to be totally inefficient. These markets, in their unidealized actuality, produce countless harmful effects, and enemies of the whole market idea are naturally quick to seize upon them. In return these critics are told, if such and such a market works badly, that's because of contingent factors preventing it from conforming rigorously to the fundamental law of all true markets. This sort of debate, evidently, remains on so lofty a level of abstraction that it can contribute nothing. What is needed above all else is reflection on the underlying reasons why certain markets function badly in order to make clear the key problem of the intrinsic limits to virtue, to belief in goodness, the postulate of trust, and consensus.

The way the market functions raises two major issues that have never been clearly resolved: (1) the relation between individual desires and collective interests, (2) the tension between optimum short-term adjustment and long-term development. The model of the "invisible hand," which maintains that the first problem takes care of itself, is a striking discovery but it is often applied without rhyme or reason. Its validity has often been confirmed in economically developed societies, but not always, and it has often proved a failure in the Third World. The truth is that in order for it to work a certain number of conditions have to be met: honesty on the part of the major forces in the market, aboveboard operations from start to finish, sufficiently equal access to the market, and the possibility of negotiation. Should these conditions be lacking, the door is thrown open to all sorts of manipulation, and various well-placed individuals or groups acquire huge unearned incomes for themselves. Rich tend to get richer not only at the expense of the poor but at the expense of the system as a whole which tends to deteriorate.

As far as the even more vexing problem of the long term goes, examples abound to show that arrangements optimally suited for the short term can threaten development for the long term. Too easy is the reply that there is a market composed of all those interdependent markets (i.e., the stock exchanges or money market), which will ensure all necessary adjustments as every market does, in other words, ideally. Already simple products are highly complex feats of human engineering. Financial "secondary" markets as described by their apologists are still much harder to construct; they presuppose conscious initiatives and choices made within the framework of collective restraints.

Americans, for the most part, have a far too dogmatic faith in the virtues of "the Market." Their economic experts take a doctrinaire rather than empirical approach, and their science, whether Keynesian or monetarist, has not managed to adapt to a changing pattern of problems. In the sixties the Keynesian doctrine, decked out with certain improvements, was viewed as a monument of rationality, but when the dollar was devalued in 1971, the doctrine collapsed. As for the monetarists and other "new economists," they can raise no one's hopes, unless they stay on the sidelines, criticizing the party in power but not taking matters into their own hands. The end result of all this is that at this time nobody can put together a workable strategy for putting the American economy back on sound tracks. Here are some simple examples. The short-term adjustments made automatically by American industry lead to massive layoffs, followed, of course, by rehiring when the time is ripe. This flexibility has long been considered a powerful advantage, but the brilliant successes of Japanese and German industry have shown how illusory it was: a minimum of flexibility is obviously indispensable, but too much depreciates the work force, whose qualifications are an absolutely critical resource. The solid strength of German industry lies in the highly qualified workers whom it trains and protects with jealous care; the Japanese have an extraordinarily adaptive work force employed by stable and supportive companies. American industry is now discovering, a little late in the day, that it no longer has the human resources demanded by sharper competition, and that it will have to undertake a major retraining effort.

Another result of overconfidence in the market has been the downturn of certain industries. When, over the years, American railroads performed disastrously, people admitted it and coyly argued that, after all, the railroads worked so badly just because they were managed by the federal government, and their share of the transportation market naturally fell to the private entrepreneurs: the bus companies, truckers, and airlines. But when steel and then rubber began the same downhill slide and the auto industry seemed likely to follow, that sort of optimism ceased to be appropriate.

The dogmatic application of market principles to the internal workings of a company can lead to similarly bad results. Too fierce a competition between management executives does not in general bring about growth and innovation but a diminishing of resources. And if the egoism of different leadership groups passes a certain limit, the company is simply headed for the bottom.

Nor does the consumer necessarily profit by industrial competition. In his witty book, *Exit, Voice and Loyalty*,[8] Albert Hirschman has admirably pointed out how often on the American mass markets the products are so alike that reactions by unhappy consumers, that is, movement from one product to another, can balance out to the extent that companies simply rotate their clientele and never feel any pressure to improve their products. In fact, adaptation and innovation require a minimum of stability in company-client relations; otherwise consumers can have no say in the process of development.

The problem is particularly acute in the service sector, where the United States has seen a much more pronounced deterioration than has Europe or Japan because service markets cannot function properly without much more extensive innovations at the level of human relations. In order to function well, the person who provides the service and the one who hires it have to spend enough time together so as to understand each other and open up a learning process. But the principle of immediate optimization prevents this sort of symbiosis. To proceed by continually inviting bids, specifying each time exactly what one is looking for and choosing on a case-by-case basis the supplier who quotes the best price, is to condemn oneself to bad service. As for the suppliers, if they decide, for the sake of rapid development, to offer standardized services on the grand scale, they will unquestionably sell them at first, but their product will be less and less useful, and they will finally go under (in this area, the market for consulting and research services to the federal government offers a fine example of waste and inefficiency). America, of course, has no monopoly on this situation, but Americans seem to have a harder time than others in seeing where their problems lie. The situation is particularly serious if we think how crucially important services are in the new type of growth imposed on us by recent social change, favoring not just the work of consulting firms, think tanks, and other purveyors of advice to government and business but services of all sorts—communications, leisure activities, tourism, health, and so forth.

[8] Albert Hirschman, *Exit, Voice and Loyalty: Response to the Decline in Firms, Organizations, and States* (Cambridge: Harvard University Press, 1970).

On this score large companies, hampered as they are by their budgeting and auditing methods, seem just as inefficient as public bureaucracies.[9] Services everywhere are becoming more and more expensive (while the work force is no better paid than in Europe) and less and less efficient. Consumers everywhere are complaining. Only in the sectors influenced by the counterculture spirit of the sixties are there any signs of renewal.

Meeting and Smiling

The fundamental problem that one is forever rediscovering, beneath government structures, systems of organization, and even the troubles with the market, is that of people meeting one another. Yet in this regard no society appears to be more advanced than America. Foreigners are always struck by the naturalness and discreet efficiency with which Americans bring off momentary encounters. "Hi!—Hi!": a quick exchange, in a tone of voice faintly warmer and more cordial than usual or, frequently enough, the simplified version where a silent smile responds to another smile, or an imperceptible wink is met by another wink, as if to say, "I recognized you, I know you're there, and now you know that I'm here."

This minimal amount of information is acquired at bargain rates, which seems to be a prerequisite for functioning without loss of time or energy in an increasingly complex society. If it goes without saying that reducing meetings to a simple minimal unit of information, to a computer bit (yes/no, $+/-$, 1/0, black/white), is gravely inadequate from the human point of view, it is nonetheless impressive and, within well-defined limits, useful. When one has at one's disposal a comparable vocabulary of rapid signs, emotionally neutral and stripped of all the old connotations expressing inhibition or dependency, one can get right down to business and take joint action much more quickly, with maximum efficiency. It is what has made possible such fast-moving and coherent deployments of force as the one by students and other protesters that led to Johnson's fall. It is what gives the American working lunch its astonishing productivity.

This kind of human-relations skill, however, is not effective except when placed at the service of something other than itself within the framework of a longer term cooperation. It could never be enough all by itself to guarantee the success of any enterprise whatever. The

---

[9]The fact that the United States is largely ahead in the world for exporting services should not be taken too quickly as a sign of superiority. Competition has not really begun yet.

most important thing is not the ability to make the most of the moment but to aim farther off, to go deeper, to know how to waste time, perhaps to suffer. Americans are beginning to find out how frequently the whirlwind activity they rush about in eventually proves to be futile. Along with this discovery goes the fact that a large number of them are becoming aware of something missing, some lack they had already vaguely sensed for some time, although they have no idea how to fill the void.

Europeans who live for a while in America generally go through the same series of phases. Once the initial bewilderment has passed, they are amazed by the openness of the people. Anybody can talk to anybody. Contact is immediate, communication easy. Those Americans who so often seem incoherent mumblers communicate infinitely better than the French who are so proud of their artful self-expression. Then comes a second reaction, which is a second mistake: all that suddenly looks superficial. Americans communicate with everybody, but they have no friends, personal relations carry no weight. And then comes a third phase—uncertainty, the one in which I find myself still struggling: the fact of the matter is that, like everybody else, Americans need affection, friendship, and love. And they get it too, but it comes harder than for others, and it costs more, because they lack a code, a culture in the domain that will always be closed to the computer, that of complex human relationships. Behind the superficial openness there lies, in most cases, a request for something deeper so much so that the European thinks for a moment that he may have been too brutal. Could it be that despite his supposed civility he has boorishly neglected a whole dimension of human reality, hidden from sight, but rich in content and asking only to be put to use?

Yet upon reflection the European sees that such brutality comes from his having gone along with the system. What he has done, essentially, is play the American in America: too accustomed to the protection afforded by his habitual code of behavior, he has refused to take chances.

American futurologists who have dealt with this problem, Alvin Toffler in particular, seem to have missed completely its deeper implications.[10] As they see it, the only issue is human capacity to keep up with a changing world. One has to move faster and faster to stay

[10]Alvin Toffler, *Future Shock* (New York: Random House, 1970); see also *The Third Wave* (New York: Morrow, 1980); Herman Kahn et al., *The Next 200 Years: A Scenario for America* (New York: Morrow, 1976); Zbigniew Brzezinski, *Between Two Ages: America's Role in the Technetronic Era* (New York: Viking, 1970). Kahn and Brzezinski have in fact ignored the problem.

on top of increasingly complex problems. Lots of people are going to be left by the wayside, but that is the law of evolution. . . .

The winners, however, in this increasingly complicated contest are not the hectic, hyperactive, or uprooted characters but persons who have managed to foster their autonomy and maturity by drawing upon the resources of a living culture, that is, by developing or re-developing roots. This holds for nations as well as for individuals. Take the Japanese: as Chie Nakane has brilliantly shown in *Japanese Society*,[11] they have succeeded not because they are so modern but because they know how to find in their "backward" traditions the wherewithal for surviving in the modern world. Thus, they run their companies not at a breakneck American pace but to the slowly swelling rhythm of a "feudal" conference. Or consider the personalities who in recent years have commanded worldwide attention, especially in the media. Why does the figure of Pope John Paul II seem to burst through the television screen? Why did General de Gaulle make so good an impression on viewers far from France? The main reason is that we have here men of culture, yet solitaries, capable of slipping away from the hurly-burly and taking the time to meditate. These men, to all appearances are tied to the past and yet best suited to play the game of the future, because one does not prepare for the future by hasty day-to-day adjustments. What a contrast between a John Paul II or a de Gaulle and recent American presidents, Johnson, Nixon, or Carter—who look hopelessly immature by comparison.

David Riesman, to my thinking the best analyst of American society, anxiously wondered in an article about the rising egocentrism of young people in America.[12] He views this phenomenon as a violent rejection of older American values, an evolutionary step away from traditional individualism toward a more and more irresponsible self-fishness. The original sort of American individualism was in no way incompatible—quite the contrary—with long-term commitments, the willingness to initiate things, the thoughtful effort to build a personal and collective future, all of which are becoming impossible today because nobody wants to take any risks. The cult of spontaneity, sincerity, and self-expression has actually led to sterile conformism. In pointing out the virtues of a kind of minimal hypocrisy, which obliges one to respect both oneself and others, Riesman explains the spread of disturbing signs such as vandalism, campus theft, and teenage pregnancy, testifying to the wave of irresponsibility now sweeping over this everyone-for-himself society. The "culture of narcissism," to use

[11]Chie Nakane, *Japanese Society* (London: Weidenfeld, 1970).
[12]In "Egocentrism: Is the American Character Changing?" *Encounter* (August 1980).

Christopher Lasch's term, does not banish the terrifying solitude that reigns in present-day America; it actually makes it worse.

The same goes for the proliferation of psychoanalysis and encounter groups. For me the whole problem finds immediate physical expression in the quality of the American smile. In the good old days Americans smiled a great deal, but their smile, with its all too obvious superficiality, was hard to bear. The Japanese smile, though it also makes a painful impression on foreigners, is so patently a social mask that one almost comes to forget it is there. By contrast, the American smile back then undeniably welled up from within the person, and there was no way you could discount it. Almost sincere and at the same time an all-purpose social gesture, it asked for friendship but at once made that request ridiculous.

In the course of the student revolt, amid the sound and fury, new smiles began to appear, more natural, more human, announcing an infinitely more authentic openness to other people, a noticeable advance beyond the old conventional "everybody's-so-nice" attitude. But the time of hope has passed, and the beatific smiles have practically disappeared. There is more diversity now, of course, but the smile on the face of Americans, though it looks a little tired these days, has become no less superficial than it was before. The hippies, the flower children, those visitors from Eden who were greeted ecstatically by many American thinkers (and Europeans) had built their world on sand, and there is nothing left of it. Their goal was to make themselves deeper and to be truly open to the other, but that other was no less than everybody. Now, you have to choose: yes, it's fine to smile in a genuine, human way; and it's fine to make love. But you can't open yourself to one and all, nor make love with every human being you pass in the street, without sinking into absolute superficiality—or madness. Drugs, it is true, can keep the smile going, but at the cost of escapism and death. Drug addiction has convulsed America, not so much as a health problem or a social crisis but as a metaphysical dilemma.[13]

The Rediscovery of Evil

Europe, it may be objected, is likewise suffering from the vices of superficiality, narcissism, and irresponsibility. And so I shall be accused of being just one more crepehanger railing at the younger generation. Yet, while Europe undoubtedly has the same problems as America,

[13]The scourge of alcoholism, which has been raging for more than a century, apparently without really disturbing anyone, costs the nation at least twenty times as much as drug addiction.

everything is a matter of degree. The problem for Americans is that the country has deteriorated so badly that they do not even get indignant over it any more. The French scream in protest the moment anyone steps on their toes. Americans, however, are just now beginning to react. Isolated voices like Riesman's or of a different sort like Solzhenitsyn's have not been heeded. The fact is that their culture, the very point at issue here, disposes Americans not to react but rather to go on insisting that everything is OK and to turn the other cheek. There is no longer anyone available for the role of father for taking on the burden of maturity.

When all is said and done, what is missing in American culture? I venture to say, it is evil, or more precisely the acknowledgment that evil exists. Americans will not be able to rediscover the sense of community and public enterprise, they will not be able to rediscover any depth in their lives, unless they are willing to stretch their thoughts beyond the single dimension of law, virtue, and the consensus, because thought deals with evil differently from the way it deals with good. The problems of sin, punishment, or deterrence are in sharp contrast with those of choosing what is best, the pursuit of happiness, or respect for juridical forms.

But do we really have to raise these questions in metaphysical, rather than psychological or social, terms? Yes, absolutely, because America, a country Europeans imagine to be pragmatic and narrowly materialistic, is above all preoccupied by metaphysical choices. In Europe people naturally think in psychological and social terms. They are passionately interested in evil, they delight in psychological analyses of vice. Our criminals are deliciously complex creatures, worthy of a François Mauriac or at least of a Georges Simenon. In America no one delivers subtle discourses on evil, the only kind of philosophizing people understand concerns the roots of goodness. What is at stake, for example, in all the Westerns? The aim is nothing less than to make the world over, to reestablish the community by gathering it around a core of goodness. There may be some ambiguity in "intellectual" Westerns, but only because there the discovery of good occurs gradually, passing through uncertainty over the different possible goods one has to choose from. Evil is present, of course, but in a simplistic, stereotyped fashion, and no one asks any serious questions about it. Nor, for that matter, does anyone reflect on how the good is to be given a social basis—it will be imposed by smoking pistols. Even the Vietnam War inspired a work in this genre: the film *Apocalypse Now* is an extravagant quest for good by wading through horror until the final engulfment in the vermin-infested jungle, without anyone's taking a minute to wonder about this devolution, which transforms good into evil. From start to finish we are wallowing in metaphysics.

Europeans too are affected by this condition, quite obviously. But they have other resources. Since time immemorial they have been accustomed to seeing evil everywhere: their whole civilization and the personality of each individual have a built-in allowance for evil. In their eyes children remain creatures who have to be civilized. I do not claim that this effort has always been successful, but that after the setbacks there has been progress. Europeans gradually assimilate new behavior patterns by civilizing them. It has taken them centuries to learn how to civilize evil, and that is what makes them so complex and difficult. But it is also what enables them to respond to this fundamental problem. Sin still exists in European culture. The knowledge Europeans have of the sinner, the respect they continue to feel for him, guarantee the survival of a freedom that is no doubt more modest than the American variety but incomparably more concrete and capable of being implemented in a far richer and more lasting fashion. The ethics of sin offer a deeper foundation for freedom than the ethics of the purely formal social contract. When people suppose that evil does not exist, choice does not exist for them anymore, and freedom loses its balance. The freedom to do whatever you want without restrictions of any kind leads to narcissism, guilt, and anxiety.

The American adventure, that new creation, has brought a previously unknown dimension of experience to the rest of humanity. It has awakened the West and the whole world with it. We have all benefited immensely from this American dream, which has become our dream too. Without it we would have been doomed to rigidity and inevitable decline. In his most moving "I have a dream" speech, Martin Luther King, Jr., still could echo the traditional motif. It was still possible to try once more to lay the foundations for a new world, as Americans had always done, with their Bible and their law books. But the last frontier has already been reached. Now the task is to live with one's past and one's sins, working to civilize an evil reality that no prohibition, which by its very nature must be merely verbal, can ever destroy.

In the "time of saturation" that Americans now enter—Europeans have been there for centuries—one cannot decree a new transformation every year. This does not mean that Americans have to abandon their Calvinist faith and begin to govern their individual and collective existence in the light of Jesuit casuistry. But it is now their turn to learn the lesson they once helped others master: how to reason using two different logical systems at once.

CHAPTER EIGHT

THE
CHALLENGE AHEAD

**Big Brother's Time
Is Up**

IN THE SHORT RUN, NOTH-
ing succeeds like success.
Riches and power unfail-
ingly accrue to the rich and
powerful. But in the long run, as history teaches us, just the reverse
is true. Prolonged success always brings decline. The rich and powerful become lazy and complacent. Not only individual people, not
only groups and classes but also whole nations and societies suffer the
same fate. What we so easily admit for individual people seems hard
to admit for powerful institutions and especially for the nations and
societies to which we belong, but it infallibly happens.

There is no paradox in this contrast. As long as the conditions
that have made success possible persist, the people, groups, and societies that have succeeded by developing the talents and capacities
required for these conditions will have a decisive edge over their
competitors. But in the long run conditions always change. And one
society after another has been trapped in the same fallacy of excep-
tionalism. Societies tend to believe they have made it because of their
exceptional qualities or at least because of the perfection of their
methods. They cannot understand that the modes of reasoning that

brought them continual success in the past will be responsible for bringing failure in the future. They don't know how to move beyond the basic paradigms of their early learning and will often, unfortunately, find it easier to refuse a new reality than to adjust to it.

America's troubles are not just troubles of temporary adjustment. They are not simple problems of restoration or repair. No, they are the deep, serious matters of decline and renaissance. Like so many of their predecessors in ages past, Americans have been too ready to believe that theirs was the perfect society or, more subtly, that they had discovered the definitive formula for an endlessly perfectible society. The due-process system, the mass production–mass consumption market, the management model of rationality, and the egalitarian welfare state have been in truth conquests important for the human race. But just like other great social innovations, these should not have been crystallized into unquestionable principles of action. When this happens, as to a large extent it now has, it prevents people from understanding and even seeing the very reality they have set out to create; the implementation of hardened principles becomes counterproductive, and the system enters a phase of decline.

To meet the challenge ahead at that stage, a society must face a world which is no longer the safe and tamed world of its former successes. At such a time, it must not rush into action, for the action it knows all too well will be the kind of counterproductive action that is dictated by its own outmoded system of beliefs. It must rather slow down and try to understand the nature of the crisis it must overcome. It must pause and consider what is really at stake.

No doubt there is a crisis in America today. Business goes on as usual, of course, but no longer quite as it should. The system works only within certain limits, and people have the unpleasant feeling that these limits are narrowing around them. Proven ways do not give the expected results. Blaming nobody, often enough, Americans nonetheless expect the worst. Feelings of uneasiness are surprisingly widespread, the more intense because those who suffer them rely on traditional schemes of interpretation that simply do not fit anymore. Modern tradition tells us that a crisis ought to be either economic or social. But this crisis is neither. It is not even a crisis in the values system. It is a crisis in the American way of life and ultimately a crisis in the American mind.

Realities are not harsh per se. They are harsh because we lack the tools to master them. And they seem even harsher when we are too biased by our own traditional modes of perception to understand or even see them.

Americans are the prisoners of a logic better adjusted to the simpler conditions of former times than to the complexities of our oversocialized, overorganized, and yet illogical world. This seems hard to believe since no other country looks more "modern" or has contributed more to the coming of just such a world than the United States. But being more efficient at starting change does not mean necessarily being better prepared to adjust to the conditions brought about by change. The great superiority of the American social logic has been its capacity to mobilize energies for pioneering change as long as change meant primarily material and economic growth. The same social logic may become a drawback when change means solving problems of quality and care, and when learning processes take precedence over allocation processes.

America's still prevalent logic tends to orient people toward patterns of instant action and instant gratification, as if the individual should act unilaterally and care only about his own course, trusting that he will be rewarded by the market, by the community, or even by God in a clear and unequivocal way. An inexhaustible physical and human environment will take care of the consequences and pay the costs. Even ecologists seem to reason as if only principles should count. In no other developed country do people insist so much on their rights. Nowhere else do they defend what they consider to be right in so unilateral a way.

Such patterns fostered activity, growth, and development in the past but will most probably favor paralysis in our present context. The more people require and demand action in such a way, the more the system in which they are enmeshed will become paralyzed. Democratic allocation processes are turning into bureaucratic quagmires.

For this American logic to be successful, it was necessary that the country enjoy certain specific advantages in resources, in time, and in protection against possible impact from the rest of the world. It maintained these advantages long after the frontier was gone. But now the situation has been reversed. The United States no longer enjoys the extraordinarily favorable ratio of men to resources which it managed to maintain for three hundred years. As the land of plenty, it escaped the laws of Malthus. Americans did not have a structure themselves, therefore, in the cumbersome way of the Old World. They could grant everybody an unheard-of freedom of action and let time take care of the adjustment. This entailed a lot of waste. But in the New World, management by waste was more efficient than the forced cooperation, control, and restraint of the Old World.

The mass production—mass consumption formula was not in contradiction with this logic. Indeed it can be viewed as a development of that logic which helped the United States maintain its advance. The structures that were developed may have been antagonistic to the American pioneering spirit, and yet in and of themselves they still obeyed the simple traditional logic.

For such a system to work, two conditions were required, conditions that have now disappeared: first, a sizable disparity of resources vis-à-vis the nearest possible competitors; second, the absence of political, military, and economic entanglements with these competitors. The country which pioneered free competition and the open market was as a matter of fact protected from external affairs much better than any European country had ever been, for all the European economic tariffs and regular standing armies.

How ironic to discover the complete reversal of perspective that has been forced on the United States now! The nation that complains loudest about the impossible burden imposed on its resources by military expenditures and foreign entanglements is the American nation.

For long, America was protected from the constraints nature imposed on other, more settled countries. But, here again, there has been a subtle reversal. By all accounts, America seems now to feel such constraints more acutely than small, densely populated nations like Belgium and the Netherlands.

Meanwhile, other Western countries and Japan have more or less caught up with the American standard of living; the wage differentials that had remained stable for three hundred years have all but disappeared. A completely different kind of competition has set in. The United States cannot win just by feeling freer as regards the use of its resources. Resources themselves, after all, are less and less natural: they are part of a world power system. Management and government by waste is no longer possible, much less efficient. Choices are required: "guns and butter" has given way to "guns *or* butter." Finally America's entanglements with the rest of the world have produced an unheard-of situation according to which Big Brother has become the prisoner of his allies and his clientele and has lost most of his freedom of action.

American logic—based on simple good-and-evil formulas and on simple patterns of adjustments and resource allocations that cannot easily deal with complex systems and do not allow for longer learning processes—is especially ill fit for such a world.

Big Brother was a wonderfully nice fellow so long as his resources made it possible for him to reward and punish friends and enemies without having to suffer from it. But now that he has to worry about consequences, he becomes demanding and unpleasant, widely resented and ever more easily manipulated.

The New Nature of the American Case

Two contradictory statements are equally valid and central for understanding the American crisis: *America's plight is not hers alone,* it is the common plight of all postindustrial Western societies confronted with a strange new world whose complexity they cannot master; *America nevertheless is still a very special case* because its rigidities are of a different nature, because its commitment to the dominant mode of rationality remains deeper and stronger than that of other postindustrial countries, and, finally, because its sheer size and power impose specific constraints it cannot discard.

I have already sketched some of the major problems all our postindustrial societies have to face. In all of them the number of people participating in any given decision affecting the common good has increased enormously as has the number of points of view taken into account. Computers, whatever else they can do, are no substitute for bargaining. The superiority of our open systems are on trial because open systems are in fact superior only if they can regulate themselves. When they cannot do so properly, they enter spirals of disintegration and decline. To maintain themselves they have to improve, but they will not improve without constant efforts at institutional creativity. They were effective formerly because of the existence of social barriers, religious taboos, and elitist traditions. As these nondemocratic props of democratic rule decline, other modes of regulation have to develop. These may be less costly in material and moral terms, but will they develop in time? The prevalent shift toward apparently easier—bureaucratic, impersonal solutions—only increases the complexity of the system and further decreases our capacity to master it.

The general impression of confusion and drift that seems so depressing in America today is not wholly specific. It is felt all over the West. The record of past civilizations and especially of our Western progress shows quite a number of similar periods of confusion. The myth of the Tower of Babel exemplifies some basic contradictions of human societies. Confident in their enterprises, they set out to build the ultimate tower, then reach a point when they cannot master even their own relationships. People cannot talk to one another anymore and are forced to part. But if one tower has to be abandoned, another may be built later. The human race has always been able to find ways. Of course in the process a great many human groups—tribes, cities, and nation states—have declined or disappeared when they could not find the right answer in time. But others made it. Why should we not be able to make it also?

It can be argued that our risks are greater now because we have become one world and this very unity renders us vulnerable. But at the same time we enjoy many advantages and capacities our ancestors did not have. Our reflective capacities have increased, and the range of experiences available to us is extraordinary. Societies may no longer be independent enough to strike and succeed alone, but they retain their capacities to experiment, and lessons can be drawn from the results of their different approaches. There is a measure of hope in the recognition of the commonality of our problems: not that we are all going to merge in the same impersonal brave new world but only that our experiences now are much more comparable precisely because they are solutions to the same problems. Because we have different resources, different know-how, different strengths and weaknesses, our innovations will be different. To succeed now, however, one cannot strike it alone. Complacent self-contained and isolationist societies are bound to lose. More open societies better able to learn will draw more easily from the rich pool of solutions that have been experimented the world over. It is less the solutions that are lacking than the capacity, the will, and the humility to understand them and take advantage of them.

From such a broadened perspective the American case appears paradoxical. From a strictly rational point of view, the United States should have been in a much better situation than any other developed democratic country to pioneer for change. Indeed this is what most experts have taken for granted. Even now American resilience, the American capacity to rebound and solve any problem if given a little time remains for many almost an article of faith.

Yet if one looks closely enough at the present situation, the picture one gets is widely different. Not only will we get an impression of confusion and drift but also this pervasive feeling of a sort of numbness if not of atonement. This seems not to be the time for intense, socially constructive activity. People worry but they don't change. Worst of all, they are less curious than at any time since World War II. Never before has there been so little interest in foreign experiences. Never before has there been so little receptivity to new ideas. Never before have young people been so self-centered and America-centered.

It is saddening for this author, as a Frenchman, to hear and read the comments of harassed and anxious Americans who seem to behave as Frenchmen did consistently thirty years ago to maintain their self-esteem in an unhospitable world. From early childhood on I heard the constant rehashing of standard complaints about smart foreigners exploiting our French scientific discoveries and technological break-throughs to develop new consumer goods, industrial processes, and marketing systems that would undersell our national industries and put our workers on the dole. Similarly, Americans now review all new achievements just to discover how many of them have been stolen from America. From computer chips to industrial robots, from lasers to quality circles, they complain about the unacceptable practices of these unfair competitors who use American innovations to outcom-pete America. "What US pioneers, other nations perfect," reads a Washington *Post* headline. Aggressive Japanese and even greedy Eu-ropeans are perceived as materialist intruders who use their mercan-tile tricks unscrupulously to outcompete the more disinterested and research-minded Americans. As if superior knowledge in marketing, production, and finance had not been the universally acknowledged reasons for the prodigious American successes of the last hundred years.

Resentment does not help understand reality. It leads to scape-goating; and besides the Japanese villains, there seems to be quite a cast of villains in present-day America: corporations that sell America's superiority for short-term monetary benefits, labor unions that price American labor out of the market; Washington bureaucracies that paralyze business and stifle innovation with all their rules and regulations.

These regressive reactions may be only temporary. Nevertheless they signal the very difficulty which America has in facing its prob-lems. What is so disturbing is not the discovery of limits and loss of power, even of failure per se. It is rather a basic change of perspective; in effect, a challenge to the national identity.

Traditionally the American case was the unique case, to be under-stood differently from all others, not by looking back to history but by looking ahead to history's promises. America was the place where the existential problems of the future were to be argued, where prob-lems were to be explored and solutions tested. Other countries were observers. Later they would implement according to their own views and at their own pace what had been achieved in mankind's main laboratory. Meanwhile their leading specialists were welcome to drop in, pick up new ideas, new fashions, catch the trend. Other countries had problems of one sort or another. They had their history. But America—America was where the action was.

In the distribution of roles among nations Americans were eager to recognize that Germans could be better craftsmen, Englishmen better citizens, and Frenchmen better artists or better cooks. They did not care. They knew they had a much more important role: they were to be the explorers of the future. This was not mere naive pride, this was the recognized judgment of scholars over time. Tocqueville more than anybody else succeeded in turning this logic to intellectual advantage by using the American case as the basic paradigm for understanding the future of democracy everywhere.

Nobody would dare use the American case today as the lab for the future. If anything, the country is taken as a warning. The future cannot be discovered in the prevailing patterns of this or any more advanced country. Americans may still explore and achieve as many "firsts" as any others, but their patent on exploration has expired.

Nations do not accept drastic change easily. When they have been long enough in the limelight, they have a hard time adjusting to a less glorious common fate. Americans have especially enjoyed their Big Brother role. Even if they resented being exploited and abused by their weaker partners, they loved to recount their explorations into the future. Paradoxically enough, the American case may remain indeed a special case not because America will regain its status as the laboratory of the future but only because Americans will take so long a time to adjust to the fate of being just another land struggling with the turbulent present.

In this predicament, the burden of leadership—which Americans will not be able to discard for a long time—will be another factor preventing them from seeing the issues as clearly as they should. They are still the obvious leaders but no longer because they are more advanced, richer or more skillful but only because their size, relative isolation, and history still hold them in this role.

The New Frontier Is the Frontier of the Mind

More than any other people in the civilized world, Americans overemphasize action. Looking decisive for them remains the only way to be taken seriously.[1] In this regard, American radicals join hands with the most conservative American businessmen: even feminists in America tend to adopt spontaneously this quasi-macho posture. In many circumstances, however, one is tempted to tell them: "Act less, think more." Most often, as a matter of fact, real leadership does not side

[1] Emphasizing action and decision is perfectly compatible with the fear of decision I have discussed in chapter five. The more people shy away from the risk of difficult decisions, the more likely they are to strive hard to look "decisive."

with forceful decision making but with courageous questioning and imaginative understanding; jumping into action prevents us from seeing realities and helps perpetuate the problems it was supposed to solve. We will not get out of the contradictions and vicious circles by forceful action alone but by resorting to the only basic human resource: human intelligence. Changes happen neither by God's special decrees nor by government decisions. They are engineered by human art, which means intelligence and care of the many not just rational decisions from the few.

This has always been true. Our ancestors would not have come out of the confusion of the Tower of Babel had it not been for the elaboration of new methods for working together, which were of course a product of trial-and-error processes but must be viewed also as an operation of the mind, endowing the human species with its unique capacity to overcome circumstance.

What must remain speculation for a remote past becomes something more than speculation as we enter historic times. The modern seventeenth-century rationalist state followed on the learning explosion of the Renaissance just as the liberal bourgeois development of the nineteenth century was made possible by the intellectual revolution of the Enlightenment. And French historian Georges Duby has argued convincingly that the tremendous pioneering development of the early Middle Ages was made possible by a basic conceptual revolution that brought about a new model of rationality.[2]

This is to an even greater and clearer extent what we are confronted with now. The religious and political framework in which these issues were debated formerly and which obscured them has become irrelevant, and soon so will the political quarrel between liberals and conservatives. Our new frontier now is no longer political or even social: *it is the frontier of the mind.*

Our fate will not be determined by the mere will to determine it, by mere decisions about the urgent problems of today. It will depend much more on the development of the capacity of our people to use their collective intelligence to master the problems. For making this development possible, we will have to rely on more effective intellectual schemes, for which we need new models of rationality and new patterns of interaction and learning. To allocate more public goods and more rights to more people in an egalitarian way is not enough. It may even be counterproductive if they cannot cooperate to take advantage of them because their capacities to learn and to

[2]Georges Duby, *Early Growth of the European Economy.*

interact are poor. To overcome its present impotence, the United States—like other developed countries—has no other course than to invest in knowledge and understanding and in the institutions, formal and informal, which make knowledge and understanding possible.

The saddest thing about the present plight of the Western world and especially of the United States is not its relative impotence in maintaining its liberal creed in a shrinking world, it is its strange intellectual demise, its lack of enthusiasm for the intellectual pioneering of the future. The American way of life has become "the ratrace"; and as one recent bumper sticker reads, "The race is over: the rats won."

America has to wake up to this deeper reality. The problem is not the arms race or the pursuit of equality. It is first of all the mobilization of active intellectual resources. American successes in the post-World War II era were made possible by tremendous investments in knowledge, investments that had been pursued continuously for twenty years. The United States invested in big science for the war effort but more basically it invested in people: brilliant refugees from Central Europe, newly trained experts in all fields, a generation of college students on the G.I. bill. America managed to give a tremendous momentum to academic and scientific expansion, which led to a new model of development based on science and technology and behind it a new model of rationality which may have become obsolete quickly but was a crucial first step.

Where is that enthusiasm and drive now? America still spends tremendous amounts of money. But it is all just quantitative research allocation, not real investment, which in these matters more than any others should be investment in quality, in people, and in the institutions that could promote them.

No wonder young Americans look apathetic and sound cynical. The paradox is appalling. Everybody talks about science and technology. Yet the best students go into law and business. One hears endless reports about the consequences of the information revolution, but most young people are cynical about *all* progress, *all* change. It is as if they think that whatever will happen will happen without their taking part in it.

In the mass production–mass consumption society, the name of the game was quantitative resource allocation. This does not work in the postindustrial society in which we are moving. When services, information, and education become the key activities, the game changes. Of course quality will not replace quantity, nor will care replace control overnight. But there is no way of eluding the problem: we will have to elaborate new logics and new models of rationality in which quality and care will not be stifled by quantitative allocation and controls.

Japan already has moved in this direction. Its successes prove that one can have a more complex model of rationality where two logics at least can operate efficiently at the same time: the logic of impersonal calculus and the logic of human care. However, to discuss the Japanese case by emphasizing their special advantages of low salaries, worker discipline, and high motivation seems ludicrously inappropriate. What is striking is that nobody would have expected that these well-known special advantages, all of which existed before, would have enabled them to build a more modern economy than that of the West. Japanese success came neither from great leadership using the perfect blueprint nor from the mechanism of economic laws. It came from the widespread enthusiasm and countless efforts of the Japanese themselves who were actively involved in the use of their intelligence to develop their collective capacities.

Clearly America cannot use the same motivations but this is not the problem, the problem is to mobilize the efforts of its people. America was doing quite a lot of that in a more elitist way thirty years ago when the qualitative development of the American education and research system was at its peak. Unfortunately, after the student rebellion, liberalism turned sour. Something essential then was lost; namely, the capacity to use the energy, drive, and inventiveness of the younger generation as a motor for change and development. Only by understanding how that capacity was lost can Americans hope to recapture it.

One of their basic problems in that respect is a problem of social identity. Intellectuals, especially liberal intellectuals, complain bitterly about the reemergence of one of America's traditional curses: anti-intellectualism. For them it is one of the main obstacles to development. There is a lot of scapegoating, I am afraid, in this attitude. Anti-intellectualism is a genuine reaction which should be properly understood. It has the crucial value of a signal. Any kind of intellectual establishment has to be elitist. It cannot pretend to be otherwise. And yet elitism should not turn into intellectual arrogance, as it can all too easily, given its prevalent mode of rationality. Intellectuals are indispensable. They provide the conceptual tools that make it possible to act in new ways. They have, however, no special privilege that could entitle them to *impose* goals and values or shame others for not thinking well. Intellectuals can help people only if they respect them.

During all these years of turmoil and pain, American intelligence has shied away from the risk and challenge of other human experience in other countries as well as from the risk and challenge of the American reality. It has deluded itself in the dream of universality and perfection. To play its basic and indispensable role, America will have to come back to the humbler realities of institution building and leadership.

Nothing succeeds because it is right and well-thought-out in the abstract. To be translated into reality it must be acted upon collectively through institutional systems that are, yes, open to change but at the same time are capable of maintaining the required amount of cooperation and support among their members and partners. Institution building is essential for overcoming our present difficulties. People will not learn new patterns in the abstract. They will only invent, innovate, and learn in real, concrete situations, within human systems that will support them and be available to experiment.

None of this will develop without leadership. No innovation has ever happened without individuals taking the lead. Present-day America worships "celebrities." It loves the glamour and showmanship of prominent persons, but basically it rejects leadership. For most Americans leadership means the risk of arbitrary power, the risk of dependence, the risk of inequality. These are certainly risks but the long term risks of the other course are much more dangerous. Without commitment and care nothing can be built that will have a chance to last. And there won't be commitment and care without the assertive power of individual leadership; in other words, of individual leaders willing to run the risk of failure and the more basic risk of freedom itself.

INDEX

Designer: Dana Levy
Compositor: Publisher's Typography
Printer: Edwards Bros., Inc.
Binder: Edwards Bros., Inc.
Text: Baskerville
Display: Baskerville